EX NIHILO
Out of nothing...

An autobiography of
Dr. R. L. White, Jr.
and, A Rise to Prominence

Ex Nihilo

My motivation for writing this book is to give my testimony concerning how God's destiny for us is amazing when we manage to learn why God made us. As I allow my mind to look at the conditions under which I was born, the theological term ex nihilo, meaning "out of nothing," comes to mind. This is the phrase used to describe how God created the Heavens and the Earth out of nothing, and God has done the same for me—bringing about something wonderful where there was previously nothing wonderful to speak of. I consider how life was for me as a child; it was painful to barely have enough to survive. Yet God always made a way when there was not even enough food in the house. As life began to evolve, I slowly began to recognize the fact that God already had a destiny for my life. When I consider this fact, that God already had planned where I would end up, I hope to show the readers of this book how an unfailing faith can work miracles in your life to bring untold numbers of people into a right relationship with God when you submit to the will of God.

International Standard Book Number:

978-1-940786-92-6

Library of Congress Catalogue Number: Available Upon Request

Printed in the United States of America

Acknowledgements

To the wife, Lorraine Jacques White, who has been my greatest supporter for over 40 years with unrestrained love.

To all my children, Patrina, Christopher, Lawrence, Eudora, and Tiffany, who had to sacrifice some of the time they would have loved to have been with me for the sake of Christ and so many times they have been my choir in revivals.

To the Mount Ephraim Baptist Church that has girded my ministry with unfailing support for 50 years.

To the loyal, dedicated staff of Mount Ephraim.

To Ms. Charlene Gilliam, who painstakingly typed this book, as well as Ms. Sandra Wall, who has been the typist for past books.

To my deceased parents, who gave me the greatest thing they could. When they had little or no money, they gave me

knowledge of a God who has been my salvation and Jesus
my Savior.

To my loving siblings Robert (deceased), Reverend J. L.
White, pastor of

Second Baptist Church, Brezial, Indiana; Reverend Ethel
White-Goodrum (Robert), pastor/founder of Move Mountain
Ministry, Decatur, Georgia; Reverend I. L. White (Lureta),
Hurricane Grove Baptist Church, Commerce, Georgia; and
Willie White (Joyce) (deceased). They have been the loyal
siblings who have provided so much love and support.

And to the many thousands of Christian soldiers who worked
so untiringly in my ministry, some who have crossed over to
the other side and others who are steadfast in the ministry,
may the power of the Holy Spirit continue to rest on you.

Foreword

I was very honored when Dr. R. L. White asked me to write the foreword for his new book, *Out of Nothing*. Dr. White is one who had to overcome many difficulties during his lifetime. I have known this man of God over 35 years (as of the writing of this book), and I have witnessed firsthand how God has elevated him because of his faithfulness.

Out of Nothing details experiences of pain, shame, condemnation, and humiliation that no person, especially a child, should have to endure. This book details that life is not always easy but is filled with trials and tribulations that we must go through. Born in a small town called Dudley, Georgia, son of a sharecropper, with little or nothing to eat many times, he survived. Dr. White knew that he did have control over how he would allow God to work in his life.

His lot in life served a purpose that was yet to be realized. He did not allow fear, doubt, or challenging circumstances to keep him from becoming who God meant for him to be. He did not know then that God had a purpose for his life, but he was ready to follow the leading of the Lord.

Getting through tough times is all about placing your trust and faith in God, which will give you a purpose and a reason for living. Dr. White found out that faith is not some philosophy, but faith is confidence in which we hope for and the assurance that the Lord is working, even though we cannot see it. Faith knows that no matter what the situation in our lives or someone else's, the Lord is working in it. The Lord was working in every situation in Dr. White's life in order that God would receive the glory. Regardless of what we think, God always knows what is best for us, and there are times we must see by faith and not by our natural eyes. Dr. White found out that faith will see you through.

Living in faith and not by sight means that you are willing to go into the unknown. It is trusting God even though you do not know where He is leading you or what the outcome will be. Dr. White did not know how life was going to turn out for him or where God was leading him. All he knew was that God was at work, and he had to wait patiently to see the outcome.

The Bible tells us in Jeremiah 29:11-13, "I know the plans I have for you. . . . plans to prosper you and not to harm you, plans to give you hope and a future. Then you will call upon me and come and pray to me, and I will listen to you. You will seek me and find me when you seek me with all your heart" (NIV). Dr. Charles Stanley explains that there is no such thing as coincidence, luck, or good fortune. God is sovereign, and He has a course that He wants you to follow. He opens and closes exciting doors of opportunity, but it is up to you to step through each one by faith. You do not have to miss another exciting moment. You can live each day with a sense of hope and assurance that whatever comes our way has passed through God's omnipotent, loving hands.

This book reminds us that it is not where you start but where you end up. In Dr. White's life, we see that no matter how many times people try to defeat or crush us, God's purpose will not be impeded. When we let go of our plans, we will discover that God's plans are amazing.

I highly recommend this most exciting book.

Rev. Clarence Moore

Pastor, Good Shepherd Baptist Church, Augusta, Georgia

Former President, General Missionary Baptist Convention of Georgia

Former Southeast Region Vice President, National Baptist Convention, USA, Inc.

Introduction

My motivation for writing this book is to give my testimony concerning how God's destiny for us is amazing when we manage to learn why God made us. As I allow my mind to look at the conditions under which I was born, the theological term *ex nihelo*, meaning "out of nothing," comes to mind. I consider how life was for me as a child; it was painful to barely have enough to survive. Yet God always made a way when there was not even enough food in the house. As life began to evolve, I slowly began to recognize the fact that God already had a destiny for my life. When I consider this fact, that God already had planned where I would end up, I hope to show the readers of this book how an unfailing faith can work miracles in your life to bring untold numbers of people into a right relationship with God when you submit to the will of God.

I hope to show how the Bible can and will bring about a miracle in your own life when you avail yourself to the Holy Spirit's movement. God has allowed His calling in my life to touch literally millions of lives and has brought me the joy that can only come from a faith walk with the Lord. From humble beginnings God raised up a man out of nothing and gave him stature among the saints of God; that is nothing less than a miracle.

Table of Contents

CHAPTER ONE

Beginnings

In order for one to appreciate my assertions, he/she would have to know the circumstances under which I was born. One would have to realize what conditions were like in the deeply rural areas in the South 75 years ago.

I was born in a little country town called Dudley, Georgia, beside a railroad track. The only doctor we knew of was called a midwife. The conditions were, at best, not those that would encourage one to ever believe he/she could ever become a leader in this country.

My father was a preacher, and our only means of survival was for him to work as a sharecropper. A sharecropper would sign on with a white farmer who would supply all the material and land needed to farm the land. The sharecropper would supply all the labor, and at the end of the harvesting season, they would split the profit. On the face of it, it sounds like a fair deal, but the problem is that there was no way the laborer could verify the figures. The owner often wanted to make sure he had good workers to come back for the next season, so he had to engineer a balance due. He was seldom honest with the profit/loss reality.

Every year, my father was brokenhearted because it meant we had to go through another winter without money to sustain our meager way of life. We often went days without any food, clothing, or other necessities needed to survive. I remember my father saying once, "I am going to town and somebody is going to give me some money to buy some food for my family." I don't know what he did, but when he came home, to our joy, he had two bags of groceries.

My first remembrance of that type of life was when we moved into a dilapidated farmhouse that had been occupied by a woman who had passed away and who loved snakes. After her death, the snakes were scattered, and we moved into the house without knowing about them. The snakes would come back, and this was a fearful time for us, living in a place where we were constantly fighting snakes. I remember when one snake climbed up in a hedge right outside the kitchen window. It was horrific, and someone had to help us kill the snake.

We would often have to move at night so that the owner would not know we were gone. Because of my father's deep sense of right and wrong, he was afraid the white owner would seek to punish him if he attempted to leave. He was a good worker. He was partly angry and hurt and he would rather leave at night than face the owner who was already vindictive. Dad finally gave up on farming and moved us into a town called Dublin, Georgia, 12 miles away from Dudley. Work was scarce there too. The only jobs he could get were construction work, such as digging ditches, which paid very little.

My father pastored little churches that could only give him a little change on Sundays. They had a practice called "pounding the pastor." This meant that when they could not pay the preacher, they would make it up in vegetables and other needed food for the preacher's family.

When their family members died, he was often asked to eulogize the deceased family members. Unfortunately, the business owners who were his bosses would refuse to allow him the time off and would ask him, "Are you gonna preach or work?" So many times he would quit the job rather than let his members down. He would travel to different towns looking for jobs. I remember him going to Griffin, Georgia, looking for work, but to little avail.

My mother would do domestic work where she was paid $3.00 per day. My mother could do more with $15.00 a week than anybody I have ever known. She was the secret weapon that was always there for her family. To earn a little more money, we would go pick cotton or onions. Cotton paid $3.00 per hundred pounds and the whole family put our little money together just to make ends meet.

When I was eleven years old, in 1955, my father decided to move the family to Macon, Georgia. It was there I began to become aware of the way things really were. Because of such humble beginnings, my clothes were substandard and I often wore hand-me-down clothes. I was often laughed at by my classmates. I remember being in Ms. Linder's class in elementary school; she wanted everybody to shine their shoes before coming to school. I didn't have any polish and I tried to wash them off, but to no avail. I was ashamed and laughed at by my classmates. Ms. Linder felt so sorry for

Memorable Place: Where we lived 832 Elm Street, Macon, GA

Memorable Place: Where we lived 933 Ash Street, Macon, GA

me that she asked me to rake her lawn for a quarter so that I would have a little money to spend.

By the age of 12, I would sell *Grit* newspapers and Blair products. I realize now that people would buy my products not because they wanted them, but because they felt sorry for me. My brother Johnny had a job shining shoes at Moon's Barber Shop, and when he quit, I took over that job shining shoes for 15 cents a pair. If I did well, I got a 10-cent tip. The Reverend M. E. Moon owned the barber shop and one day he said to me, "You don't have to come back next week." I never did understand what I had done wrong. When my father asked him, he relented and told him I could come back. Even at that age, I had enough pride not to go back. I kept searching for another job shining shoes and finally found one at Statham's Shoe Repair. I stayed there until I finished high school.

Now I can look back on the painful childhood I experienced as God's personal plan for me to learn the virtues God meant for me. God wanted me to understand that the destiny He planned for my life would be one that could empathize with people with such meager beginnings. He wanted me to be able to let them know, regardless of where one begins, with God on their side, they can still make it. Wherever I am today, it came "out of nothing." Only God could do what He has done for me.

My Education

One must recognize the tremendous impact parents have on their children. Having grown up in a family that was not highly educated, my father only went to the 7th Grade and my mother was about the same. They had been raised in homes that were agrarian, which is the way they made a living. They had to help with the farming and were often kept out of school to help harvest the crops. Still, they made the best of the education they had. My great grandfather was a slave, and he made sure my dad would stay home from school to help with the farm. My mother was also under the same situation, but together they made sure we kids had at least a high school education.

R. L. White, Jr. High School Photo

My first school experience was in the Sandy Ford church school where all the grades were in the same room. I will never forget Ms. Iris. She taught all of the classes. Our only textbooks were the old books that the white school threw away. I was the smartest kid in the class and was skipped from the second grade and moved to the third grade. Consequently, I later finished Ballard Hudson High School a year early in Macon, Georgia. No one told me about how student loans work, about study jobs, or school counselors, and even though my parents would have helped me, they were still struggling, and I could not see taking the little money they had, so I opted not to continue school. I ended up staying home with my mom and dad.

Marriage and Work

I got married, but was not able to afford a home for me and my new wife, so we stayed with my mom and dad. I wanted so much to take care of my own home and I figured if I moved away from Macon, God would help me take care of my family. It was an act of faith because all I had was an old 1956 Chevrolet, less than $200, my wife, and my first child, Patrina. We moved to Washington, D.C.

The only person 1 knew there was my first cousin, who was in the dump-truck hauling business. He hauled dirt for a company owned by his uncle, Griner Cummings. My first cousin had rented us a room from an elderly woman, which worked out until the winter came. During the winter, construction work slowed down, and there were days we were not able to work at all. I remember one week I only made $19.00. There we were in this big city with only $19.00. Some of the other drivers would go on unemployment, but it was hardly enough to support my financial needs.

I had become friendly with the owner of a big building at 128 C Street N.E., right across the street from the Old Senate Building. He liked me and agreed to let me work part-time. It was hard and dirty work. The other drivers would tease me when they saw how hard I worked, and how dirty l was every day. But on paydays I would get them back by showing them the big money l was making. When that job was finished, they laid me off. I then went to the unemployment office, which in turn sent me to the post office. At that time, the post office would hire temporary workers. I loved the job, but it was only a 90-day position. I began to inquire about how to become a permanent employee, and I was told that if I could pass the civil service examination, I could stay. However, the civil service examination was closed in D.C. I later learned that the civil service examination was being administered in Hyattsville, Maryland, and it was open. I signed up to take it there and I passed it the first time. I was eventually hired.

The significance of this fact is that I had begun to doubt my ability to be smart enough to pass such an examination. I was so impacted that I started taking tests to see if I could pass them. I did not know what God was doing, but He was leading me to my destiny "out of nothing." God was preparing me for things I couldn't handle. Later, when I was called to preach, my pastor required me to go to school. It was the best thing he could have required of me because it opened my mind about education. I spent a year at the Washington Baptist Seminary and it was a blessing.

Class at Washington Baptist Seminary (R.L. - 2nd left)

Further Education

Later, when my job transferred me to Atlanta, my thirst for education had been whetted. I became a student of many classes that led to Baptist Associations. While I learned much, there was no accreditation. I then made a decision that I would never take a class again that was unaccredited. I wanted to get into the Interdenominational Theological Center (ITC). I was informed that 1 would need an undergraduate degree. I started as a part-time student at Morris Brown College, but I decided it would take too long to graduate and then go to ITC. I learned that I could enter into ITC as a probationary student if I had at least an associate liberal arts degree.

I was informed that Luther Rice Seminary in Jacksonville, Florida, offered degrees but was not accredited through the Southern Association of Accredited Schools (SACS). In the meantime, I decided to attend the Atlanta Junior College to acquire the liberal arts requirements for ITC. I ended up attending Luther Rice Seminary and Atlanta Junior College at the same time. I fulfilled the requirements at Luther Rice Seminary and graduated with the degree they awarded me to satisfy the requirements for me to get into ITC. I then decided to finish the associate degree at Atlanta Junior College so that l could have an accredited liberal arts degree. It was enough to get into ITC, but I reasoned that it would have more weight upon my study at ITC. I was able to stay on the dean's list at both schools for the duration of my studies there.

In 1985, while Dr. Ed Wheeler was dean of Morehouse School of Religion, I was inducted into the Theta Phi Fraternity, elected as the Nation Alumni president of ITC, where I served for the next 29 years. While there I achieved an MDiv degree and earned a DMin degree in 1987 and 1996 respectively. I became the first person in my family to have an advanced degree. Throughout my educational career, I knew it was not of my own abilities, but it was God moving me to achieve a successful education that started "out of nothing."

Before I was convinced to go to school, I had organized my church, the Mount Ephraim Baptist Church, which had become successful. I had decided not to go back to school because it was taking so much of my time. I had a hometown classmate whose name was Dr. Mattie Coleman; he counseled me to go back to school. I told her at that time I didn't think I needed it, and I thanked her for her advice. Today I hope she knows how she helped me to focus on the need to become educated. If there is one thing I have learned, it is the fact that one who stands before God's people to proclaim the Word of God must avail themselves to a school of higher learning. I say this knowing how difficult it is for some preachers and pastors to go to school. Now there are schools that have online programs for ministers. One can get a quality education while in the home laboratory. Whatever the case may be, I encourage all preachers to go to school.

It is not a mandatory thing for Baptist preachers to have a degree in biblical studies, but we have to realize that the people in the pews are now well educated, and they appreciate a pastor who values a good education and encourages his parishioners to become the best at whatever they do in serving the Lord. We cannot, however, dismiss the informal education of many ministers. There are some preachers who have not gone to seminary but are armed with common sense. The overwhelming number of preachers that came from a heritage of majoring in the Word of God have done some marvelous works in the service of the Lord. We can never disdain the effectiveness of preachers for hundreds of years. When higher education was almost nonexistent, we leaned on the inspiration of the Holy Spirit through the preacher and we have come this far by faith.

When a minister is divinely called by God and that minister further prepares for ministry through school, it means that he is sharpening the tools God has already given him/her. Ministers tend to be more effective with both the call and the education.

My success in ministry was different than many ministers before I went to school. I organized Mount Ephraim Baptist Church, which started with 13 members and grew to 14,000 members when I went back to school. I already had name recognition, as I had published sermons and singing CDs and appeared on national TV shows on the BET Network. Often the faculty members and my fellow students would ask me, "You are already successful; what are you doing here?" My reply was, "I want to keep it." That remark was in recognition that the typical member in the pew is more educated now and deserves more enlightened leadership that can communicate with both the learned and unlearned.

I would recommend to upcoming preachers, if there is any way they can avail themselves to seminary training, then they need to do so. All preachers should be deliberate about allowing their ministries to be led by the Holy Spirit in order to please God.

The Call

In the Baptist denomination, there is a strong belief in *the call* to preach, given by the Holy Spirit. Often it seems that if a father were a minister, the sons would become ministers too. Many will mistake *the desire* to preach as a call from God. While many denominations have an educational requirement, Baptists require a "trial sermon," sometimes referred to as an initial sermon. It is believed that if a person has not heard or has missed the call, it will show up at the trial sermon. It seems that many of the most effective preachers have been reluctant preachers. There were some quiet feelings in my family that some of my family members had more desire than calling.

My grandfather had five brothers, and they were all preachers. Both of my grandfathers were preachers. My father was a successful pastor who pastored for more than 60 years. It may be ironic that four of my parents' children are preachers, including me, and I have a daughter who is a preacher, a son-in-law who is a preacher, and two nephews who are preachers. Oh, my wife is a preacher too.

I believe my family must be related to the Levitical tribe of Israel. The Levitical tribe were mostly concerned with the moral laws of the Jewish temple. They were considered as the religious tribe since their venerated prophet Moses was from the Levitical tribe and he was trusted by God to be responsible for the righteous laws of the Old Testament. When I think about how the Lord has given my family great responsibilities to make God's laws known to the world and to tell them about Jesus, who has done so much for us all, I am honored that God has given us such an honor to carry His Word. As for me, while I consider it a blessing that God had called me to preach, I was not necessarily looking to be a preacher. But the call was on my life.

The White Family (R.L. - bottom left)

As a child, I was taught by my mother to sing, and I fell in love with gospel singing. My sister and brothers and I began singing together as a group. My mom named us the White's Four Gospel Singers. Whenever my dad would preach, my mom would get us to sing. We began to be called on at associations and religious meetings to sing. Then my youngest brother was born, our name was changed to the White's Five. When my oldest brother, Johnny, went to the army, our group stopped singing.

I wanted to sing, so I organized a group called the Angels from Heaven. There were four boys and two girls, and we became known in the Macon area and were called on in many places. We had two handicaps. One was, none of us were old enough to drive and we could not get to our engagements unless we paid someone to take us. I was always the manager of the group and I would walk the streets to find people who owned an automobile and would pay them four or five dollars to take us to sing.

The other handicap was that we had a guitar player named Abraham Lockett who was good for the group; however, we could not depend on him. Because he was not dependable when we went to sing, we would ask other musicians to play for us. That was when I decided to learn how to play the guitar. I bought an old ragged guitar and practiced every day for hours. My father told me years later that he used to wish I would put it down. After a while, I began to play simple songs. One Sunday we had a program and again we were without a musician. My sister made a statement to the group that I could play, and they actually believed her. It was the greatest compliment she could have paid me. It was on that Sunday that I became the group's permanent musician.

As time went on, the group began to move on in different directions, and only a few of us were left. I attempted to get others to join the group, but many times they would not show up for rehearsal. At that time I would borrow dad's car to pick them up, but their dedication, it seems, was gone. One evening when my father noticed how upset I was when they did not show up, he sat me down and gave me the most healing advice I had ever received. It still guides me to this day. He said, "When you have done your best, that's all you can do." He said, "There comes a time when you will have to move." That day I gave up on the group and no one ever wanted to know why.

My father was right: as soon as I gave up, I was invited to play for a teenage group called the Heavenly Wonders. They became very popular and we would do radio shows and open up programs at the Macon City Auditorium. It was then that my love for gospel singing produced a desire to become a professional gospel singer.

Leroy Scott was the biggest gospel promoter in Macon at that time. He would promote gospel programs, and we would go to every program he promoted. It was at that time I fell in love with Brother Joe Ligon and the Mighty Clouds of Joy. I enjoyed watching the Rev. Julius Cheeks and the Nightingales, the Pilgrim Jubilees, Edna Gallmon Cook, the Swan Silvertones, Sam Cook and the Soul Stirrers, the Spirit of Memphis, the Five Blind Boys of both Mississippi and Alabama, the Violinaires, The Highway QC's with Rev. Johnny Taylor, my very good friend Pastor Luther Barnes of Rocky Mount, North Carolina, and many other gospel groups. They all became my idols and I could imitate them all. It was my pleasure just to shake their hands, and I believed I had found my calling for life. I signed on with a semi-professional group and I was on my way up.

As mentioned before, when I got married but couldn't afford a place for my wife and baby, I decided to move to Washington, D.C. I joined the Central Union Baptist Church and before getting settled, I organized another gospel group and named it the Mighty Wonders, and we did well. I was always the manager for all these groups, even though the other group members were all older than me. I was moving toward my goal of being a professional gospel singer. At the same time, I had become a church deacon. When I was to be ordained, my father came to D.C. to preach my ordination sermon. His words to me were, "There is no need in them ordaining you." I asked why, and he said, "You are going to preach." This did prove to be a prophetic statement; but I only wanted to sing.

One Sunday night, my group, the Mighty Wonders, had a program at the All Nations Baptist Church that was so spiritual, I was so lifted up in the Spirit that it carried me into the next day. When I went to work, I was singing a song as I drove my postal vehicle #241405 to the Department of Agriculture to pick up the mail. On the way there, I kept singing that song. Finally I said to myself, "Why can't I stop singing this song?" It was in this moment I heard an audible voice say: "The Lord wants you to preach the gospel." For me, that was overwhelming. The call was not what I was looking for because my domestic situation had grown to be precarious. The more spiritual I had grown, the more my wife resented that growth. On one occasion, while she was upset with me, she blurted out some words: "You have been called to preach; if you preach one sermon, I will never spend another night with you." That was devastating. I really wondered how she knew that because I had told no one.

A spiritual crisis began to develop within me, and I began to be in turmoil within. I called my pastor, Reverend H. Talmadge Dean, and told him about the experience and I asked him if that were the Lord. His reply was, "I can't answer that," but he reminded me about my domestic situation, how she would never go to church with me, and said, "That's for you to answer."

For the next year or so, I would not tell anyone, but everyone seemed to know I was called. At that time I was teaching Sunday school when all the other teachers confronted me. They had discussed me and came together and asked, "Why don't you go to the pastor and admit you have been called to preach? You are preaching the Sunday school lesson every Sunday." I was stunned but still wouldn't acknowledge the call. It was like a war within me. In the meantime, I kept singing with a group and people began to ask if I were a preacher. I would respond, "No, I am just a deacon." Still I would not acknowledge the call for fear of losing my family. Besides all this, I still wanted to be a successful gospel singer.

I have to confess there was a worldly component to my hesitation to enter ministry. My theological view at the time was that a minister needs to be 100% ready to give up everything when he preaches. I also had such a dedication to my favorite football team, the Washington Redskins, at that time, and it was like I would be almost paralyzed to everything else while the game was on. I could not move until the game was over. When there were requests for programs, I would not take them until after the Redskins were off. I also loved to take my family out to different attractions on Sunday afternoon, and I had a fear of having to give that up. My theology has changed; I've realized that God has no problem with a person enjoying pleasure time with the family, or even having a favorite team, as long as it does not become one's idol.

For almost two years, I was a man in turmoil. I had no personal peace. I didn't want to let God down and I didn't want to lose my family. I would go to church and sit with the deacons and when there was an empty seat in the pulpit, it seemed to be beckoning to me. I finally decided to try the same thing Gideon did in the book of Judges in the Old Testament when God announced his call through the heavenly messenger.

Gideon placed his fleece before the Lord and the first fleece verified that it was indeed God's will for him to become the leader of Israel's deliverance from her enemies. In order to be sure God was speaking to him, he reversed the test with a second fleece and the results were the same. Then he indeed knew God was calling him.

I placed my fleece before the Lord. I have to admit I placed the fleece in a way that I thought it would say I was not called to preach. My fleece said that if I were truly called to preach, let me end up at my pastor's home without intending to go there. It was pretty easy, I thought, to avoid going there because he stayed in Northeast Washington and I didn't have anything that would require me going there. One day, I became confused trying to find 10th Street N.E. I kept being directed to different streets and wound up on Kearney Street N.E. When I stopped at the stop sign, the Holy Spirit said to me, "Look to your left." When I looked, I was right in front of my pastor's home.

Like Gideon, I said I needed another fleece. One Saturday night, I placed another fleece before the Lord. I said to Him, "Lord, if you want me to preach your gospel, let my pastor's sermon convict me of my call." The next morning my pastor opened his Bible and read this Scripture: "If any man will follow after me, let him first deny himself and follow me." It was then I surrendered my fears, my will, and my way to the Lord. It was then I made my vow to the Lord. "If I lose my home or everything, I have to preach the gospel." I made an appointment with the pastor and announced my decision to preach the gospel. He inquired about my family and what I was prepared to do. My word was, "I am prepared to do what I have to do." Pastor Dean allowed me to preach my trial sermon on my birthday, March 31, 1968.

I Still Want to Sing

My pastor had a personal idiosyncrasy: he believed that if one were called to preach, he could not sing and preach. I had been in the gospel choir and he made me get out the choir, but I still wanted to sing. I didn't tell him, but I

Heavenly Wonders (R.L. – 1st top right)

did keep my gospel group. I also knew professional singers who, in my mind, were the ultimate in the gospel world. I had become friends with them and even recorded songs that went national and made it to the Billboard charts, but across the board a hit never came.

I never understood why God was denying me my heart's desire. I wanted to be like James Cleveland and other singers who were world renown. At the same time, God just kept blessing my ministry. It was not until years later God began to answer me. He began to show me how in the end, the majority of great gospel singers end up trying to live on their reputations while the gospel world keeps on moving. But the spiritual work I am doing will be the reason that untold millions will be in heaven—because of my preaching.

The Lord gave me that revelation and showed me how effective He has made me to be. The Holy Spirit said to me, "If you had been where you wanted to be, the accomplishments you wanted would have prevented you from becoming all God wanted you to become."

Today I thank God for not making that dream come true. Although I did not make it as the big gospel singer I wanted to be, God did not take singing from me. When I came to Georgia, it was unheard of for a pastor to direct a choir. I guess l have always been a maverick. I started directing my own choir. Now, 50 years later, there is no such contention. Pastors everywhere are directing choirs.

There is a side of ministry that many pastors would rather not share, yet I believe it is incumbent upon me to share some of the pains that I have had to endure during my career as a minister of Jesus Christ. When I finally decided to accept the call to ministry, I thought the Lord would keep me from having to go through trials, and that people would always honor and accept me as a preacher/pastor. Boy, was I wrong. I soon started wearing a clergy collar to let everyone know that I was a preacher so that I would get respect. One Sunday morning in Washington, D.C., where I entered ministry, I was on my way to church and a driver hit me from behind. He got out of his automobile and threatened to fight me and said, "If you didn't have that collar on, I would beat your a**." I was in shock. When we had to go to court and he saw me coming, I didn't have my collar on. He came toward me and I was getting ready to "get it on." He then rushed to me and apologized profusely. That was a lesson to me that no one was immune to hurt but in the final analysis, God fights your battles. Nonetheless, this was small in the spiritual warfare Satan was determined to wage against me, and there were times I felt like Job.

Trials

My first marriage was not one made in heaven. While I have much respect for my first wife, who is the mother of my first three children, she was my greatest source of pain at that point in my life. I met her at a dance at the City Auditorium in Macon and was so intrigued by her beauty.

I thought very little about God's requirements for marriage. She was a thrill for my eyes and emotions. When she became pregnant, I eagerly married her because I loved her and wanted to do the honorable thing. Neither of us had any money and it became evident that with a salary of $40.00 per week I would never be able to afford a family. We got married anyway and my first daughter, Patrina, was born.

Something I was totally unprepared for was the fact that Delores, my wife, was brought up in another religious tradition. She was brought up Catholic. During the early '60s, denominations were less tolerant of each other. While my new wife was not as deeply religious as 1 was, she seemed to enjoy my gospel singing groups. A serious religious problem began to emerge. She could not appreciate how religious I was, and church just was not for her. My religious roots were so deep, and 1 had been taught that one should grow spiritually to grow closer to God. The more I began to grow in the Lord, the more she began to resent my religiosity and refused to participate in my religious practice. It was so painful for me, but I continued to grow in the Lord, and she became more resentful of my faith.

When my wife became pregnant with our third child, she was bitter because she didn't want another child. She threatened to put him up for adoption. My reaction to her was, "If that child doesn't come here, neither do you." It was a painful and difficult time for me to try to raise a newborn child without help, yet I gave it my best. My son would still have the same diaper on that I had changed at 6:00 a.m. when I returned home in the evening.

I had joined the Central Union Baptist Church and the greatest pain I experienced was when 1 became a deacon. My wife would never accompany me to the important affairs. There were two deacons who never had their mates with them: Deacon Pugh, who didn't have a wife, and me. The other families would bring their children to church and I wanted to take mine too. I would get the children dressed for church and would try to do Patrina's hair. Now that I look back on that experience, anyone could see I was not a very good cosmetologist. In fact, her hair was a bigger mess when I got through with it. Nevertheless, l was still proud of my children. Their mother would refuse to help me do her hair, but determination kept me focused on the Lord, believing that l was to train up my children in the way they should go.

When I became a deacon, she wanted no part of it, but she didn't say much. She began to notice that my love for the Lord became more and more apparent. She was so alarmed that when the Lord called me to preach, I was afraid to tell her. She refused to go to church with me. It was painful to me to see that at 14 months old, my son was not walking and not developing as he should. Before my wife and I separated, I took him home to my mother, who showed him so much love that she had him walking in a few weeks. My mother wanted to keep him with her. Later my wife asked me to bring my son back and she promised to love him. Because I believed a child should be with his mother, I brought him back to his mother and she kept her word and treated him the same as his siblings.

I am convinced the enemy, Satan, was determined to stop what would become an effective ministry that would eventually bring literally millions of people to Jesus. In the meantime, I organized Mount Siloam Baptist Church in

Washington. There was a young lady who was a member of my home church. We became great friends and since she didn't have relatives in D.C., she would often accompany me to speaking and singing engagements. It was truly a platonic relationship. Over the years, I have wished to see her again to tell her thank you for being a real friend at a painful time.

The church began to grow when the separation from my wife came. We ended up divorcing. Being a 22-year-old young man dealing with much domestic pain, I was very vulnerable. I wasn't the only one. There was an attractive young woman who had joined my church who was in a bad marriage. Because of my immaturity as a counselor, as she shared her pains, I shared my pains, and we became involved. Going through a very bad marriage was so very painful to me. My theology was, as a pastor in a broken marriage, I felt that I had let God down.

On top of all this, my job unexpectedly moved me to Atlanta. I hated to leave the church I had started. This too was very painful. The young lady and I had grown close and she said to me, "Whether you want me or not, I am moving to Atlanta." I then felt like I was obligated to marry her. She was very talented, so I felt like she could help me in ministry. She was a great help when we started the church. Again spiritual warfare showed its ugly face. Even though Mt. Ephraim was prospering, Satan kept showing up in my personal life.

My second wife had become insecure in our relationship and in 1978 jealousy began to be a major factor in our family. Many accusations began to surface and there was a continual daily argument. By then, I had begun to confide in someone else I was again where I was before I left my former marriage. Because there was no peace in my home, if I even spoke to any other woman I was guilty in her eyes and she began to believe I was doing so many things I was not doing. While I was not perfect, I certainly was not doing all she thought I was doing. She became vindictive and went to the president of the General Missionary Baptist of Georgia and told him so many things that he began to think I was a monster.

He apparently believed everything she told him because he came to my office one day while I was counseling and did everything but curse me out. I was livid, but I did not respond to him until I was calm. I told my wife to tell him that I was a professional like he was and not to come jump on me until he knew the full story.

Once, a female member called with a legitimate concern and when my wife and I would argue, she would call a mutual friend who was like a mother figure to both of us. We called her Mother Scales. On a certain Sunday night, we argued so much I left the house. She called Mother Scales and told her l had left the house to be with another woman. The truth was I had nowhere to go so l climbed in the back seat of my car and went to sleep. I was awakened when Mother Scales said to her, "He's not with a woman; he is asleep in the car."

Once I had gone to Macon to do a revival and I stayed with my parents. On that Monday night, my dad had gone to hear me preach, but I had arrived back home before him. The next day, she came down from Atlanta and was going to spend the night, but she heard me talking to and old friend—nothing she or my parents couldn't hear. When I hung up, she shouted, "So that's what you are doing down here; you were out with a woman last night." My father said, "No, he wasn't. He beat me home." She exploded and told him, "You are just cloaking for him and I will never put my foot in your house again." My parents were crushed.

She argued all the way back home and when we got in Monroe County, I said, "Shut up," and hit a passing gear. As soon as I did, the state patrol pulled me over and said to me, "I don't want any lie out of you; how fast were you going?" My response was, "I don't know how fast I was going, but I was speeding." He told me that he had clocked me at 105 miles per hour, and that he could lock me up for reckless driving. But he said that since I talked so nicely, he would let me come back and pay the ticket. He said, "If you don't, I will be at your house in Atlanta." I paid it.

On another occasion, I was in Macon in revival again; this time I stayed at a hotel. Since Macon is my home, I had spent the day with my friends. When I went to my room after church, management met me at the door and began apologizing to me. I said, "For what?" She had called my room and a maid who was cleaning the room answered the phone and identified herself as the maid. My wife raised hell, called the front desk, and told them off. I was so embarrassed.

She would jump on me and try to scratch me in my face so people would know we were fighting. I would hold her until she promised to stop fighting. When I would release her, she would start fighting all over again. On other times she would talk to my chairman of the board, telling him all kinds of things about me.

One night my children from D.C. were spending the summer with me and they were jumping off the twin beds. My wife had a knife and held Christopher as if she were going to cut or stab him. I became so incensed that I dared her to cut him and I told her what I would do to her if she did (expletive not revealed). She must have believed me, because she put the knife down. The next year after paying for them all to travel, when I went to the airport Chris was not with them. I immediately called him and asked why he wasn't with Lawrence and Patrina. His reply was, "Something told me not to come." I then realized how afraid he was to come, which was even more painful.

She was terribly insecure in our relationship and there were many arguments and accusations, and eventually she physically attacked me. I can truly say I never beat her, but I would restrain her. Once again, I was faced with the decision of becoming separated from a second wife. The good thing that came out of this marriage was two wonderful daughters: Eudora and Tiffany.

A New Beginning

In 1980, I married Lorraine Jacques from Pittsburgh, Pennsylvania, whom I had met at the National Baptist Congress. February of 2020 marked 40 years of marriage. All has not been rosy, but we are closer to each other than ever. I thank God for carrying me when I could not carry myself.

Over these years, there have been many pains that come with being a preacher for Jesus, but there is one biblical verse I have leaned on: "For he hath said, I will never leave thee, nor forsake thee. So that we may boldly say, The Lord is my helper, and I will not fear what man shall do unto me." (Hebrews 13:5-6). I hope this chapter of transparency will help other ministers who struggle with satanic attacks.

When the Bottom Falls Out

"Put on the whole armour of God, that ye may be able to stand against the wiles of the devil." —Ephesians 6:11

The one thing I had not counted on was the spiritual attacks by the devil. I was an idealist who believed that God would make sure the devil would leave me alone. The events that followed most assuredly were an introduction to the devil himself. My first wife did not immediately leave, but the difference in our way of life was very apparent. I have to say that we were not bitter at each other nor did she ever talk against me to our children. I respect her even today for being that way. We have always come together for the good of our children. She has never regretted our breakup.

I heard her say years later, "I could never have been a pastor's wife."

The devil began to make his presence felt in my personal life. Because I wanted her to participate in my faith, I wanted to make a deal with her. She used to say, "Either you take me to the club or someone else will." I would say, "If I go to the club with you, would you go to church with me?" She agreed.

At that time there was the Howard Theatre in Washington where all the famous rock stars would perform and because I didn't believe I would be recognized there as a minister, I would take her there. I have to admit I enjoyed it. She would always back out of going to church with me, but I would continue going to the Howard Theatre with her. Stars like Carla Thomas, Rufus Thomas, Little Richard, Jerry Butler, Martha and the Vandellas—almost all the famous stars would come to the Howard Theatre. But despite my giving in, she just could not accept my offer to attend worship with me. Our relationship began to deteriorate.

In the meantime, my gospel group kept singing and I would constantly be gone in service to the Lord. I was still employed at the post office and she applied for a job there too. She was hired, but had to work at night. It was so hard on her. She would sleep most of the day and didn't have the energy to cook for the kids. I would come in after getting off work and my children would be so hungry until I cooked something and they would say, "That's good, Daddy." I knew it wasn't that good; they were just hungry. It was a hard life for me.

My transportation was shaky, but I could not afford a reliable automobile. I made a deal with her that if she would agree to pay one-half of the payment, we could purchase a good automobile. She agreed, but then backed out of the deal when the very first monthly payment came around. I did not have the ability at this time to pay all the bills, and she refused to help me.

My singing and preaching ministry was growing in stature, and people just started following the group. After a while, it became the natural next step to organize this group into a church. It began to immediately grow. I named it the Mount Siloam Baptist Church. In order for me to pastor a church, I needed to be ordained. In the District of Columbia, the ministers are all from various churches in the city. If a minister had duties that warranted ordination, then and only then could he be ordained. Since I had organized a church, I asked my pastor for ordination and he was very negative. His words were, "You are about to mess up. I need to see what you are doing."

I had our members meet so we could show him our positive group. He showed up with two deacons. When we made our presentation, he said, "I don't see anything worth ordaining you for." Then he and his deacons walked out. We were pained at that statement. But I would not give up. I called my father and he called my former pastor, Rev. W. M. Hall, who knew me well. He, in turn called the minister's union in Macon. His words to my father were, "You mean they are treating my boy like that? Tell him to come home and I will ordain him."

By then I was depressed because my home was in such bad shape and on the verge of breaking up. One could just see the hand of Satan in the whole situation. I had elected a young lady in our church to be our clerk and I began to share my troubles with her. She was so sympathetic, and it was a feeling of support I had never felt before. She was married and my marriage was shaky. One day her husband hit her, and she left him. I was trying to counsel her with little experience of knowing how to counsel someone. In record time we became involved. She started demanding that I leave my "messy situation." I became spiritually paralyzed and lost all the joy I had.

Since my home situation was already getting worse and another man was taking up company with my wife, I finally left home, and I was a broken man. The thing about the attacks of Satan is, you can be under attack and not even know it. I was so depressed, I wondered if I were worthy of being called a minister, yet my young congregation was trying to be as encouraging as they could be.

In the meantime, my former pastor had called the minister's union to ordain me. I had made plans for my members to travel from D.C. to the ordination service, but I felt so unworthy—like nothing I had ever felt before. I wanted to call the service off, but so much planning had been put into the service. I showed up, not divulging my pain. Most of the ministers who were to take part in the service were preachers I had grown up around and had admired for years. They were about to ordain a preacher whose home had broken up and who was now involved with the church clerk.

The catechism went well, and all were impressed with me and with the members who had driven so far to support me. My father was asked to preach the ordination message. It was a beautiful service but, as broken as I was, I could not enjoy it. I was happy for my mother, who sat with me, and my father, who preached, which made me very happy. It was like smiling while it's raining.

I prayed to God as we returned to D.C., and I began to see the power of God's amazing grace, that God could still use me in His service. When my pastor heard that I had been ordained, he made an announcement to the Central Union Baptist Church that he was revoking my preaching license and I was no longer considered a minister from Central Union. It was painful and I could not help but feel the pain. It seemed like the devil himself was determined to stop me from preaching. There was one thing I knew: that God had called me, and God would vindicate my ministry in His own time.

Another requirement Mt. Siloam had to meet was to be recognized as a duly organized Baptist church in Washington by a council of churches. It is much like an ordination ceremony. The process was in the hands of the president of the Washington Baptist Seminary, the great Dr. Fowler, whose job was to examine the doctrine embraced by the congregation as truly "Baptist" in nature. The main question was, "How will this church be governed?" The answer expected was: The Holy Bible and the Hiscox Directory for Baptist Churches. Other bona fide Baptist churches had to be invited. Mount Siloam sailed through with flying colors and we were on our way. I began to heal and was praising God for His peace.

I just did not know what God was doing. God had already begun to move me toward my destiny in pastorship and it wasn't in D.C. Despite the fact that I loved D.C., I did not want to retire as the pastor of the Mt. Siloam Baptist Church. I had projected to be able to resign my job with the post office in five to ten years, but God had other plans. God put a person in my life that I now know had to have been an angel.

One day at the post office, this person came to me and asked if I would ever consider moving back to Georgia. I don't even know why I answered his question the way I did, but I said, "If my mother and father needed me badly enough, I would." His advice was, "It would take years to get a mutual transfer with someone else." I told him that the next time I went to Georgia, I would put in for a transfer. On my next trip, I did put in for a transfer, and to my dismay, they approved the transfer within three weeks. I was devastated. I called the post office to tell them, "I changed my mind." Their reply was, "If you want your job, you better come and get it." What I didn't know was that God was ordering my footsteps.

CHAPTER THREE

Moving to a New Address

It was on the third Sunday in October 1969 when I left Washington, D.C. to move to Atlanta, Georgia. I had stayed until the last minute before I left D.C. (around 3:30 p.m.) and I was due in Atlanta at 7:30 a.m. on Monday morning. I drove all night and arrived at approximately 6:30 a.m. I parked in a parking lot and put a note on the windshield asking the attendant to wake me up in time to go and report to personnel. The attendant complied with my request, and it dawned on me after the first day that I didn't have anywhere to live.

There was a YMCA nearby and that is where I stayed my first few nights in Atlanta. Being new to a city in which I knew no one, I began to seek a more stable place to live. I heard that the Reverend M. L. Raglin was a pastor in Atlanta. He was a pastor I had known as a child in my hometown of Macon when he had pastored the New Pleasant Grove Baptist Church. I was told that he was pastor of the First Corinth Baptist Church, so I got in touch with him. He had been my father's pastor in Macon and was happy to find me a room in a rooming house. Subsequently, I joined his church.

As I reflect back on those days, I was a broken man with not much to be happy about. My father, who was a pastor himself, had gotten me a hearing at a vacant church in a country town. (I cannot even remember the name of the town, nor the church.) When I arrived at the church, there was a mutual feeling: I did not like them, and they did not like me. I was glad to leave there. I now know that God had a special work for me, and He was directing my pathway without me even knowing what He was doing. It was during this time that I could not feel God's presence because of the pain I was feeling. I was fine with just trying to get acquainted with Atlanta.

I was assigned to the Morris Brown Postal Unit, which was in the middle of the Vine City community. This was an aged neighborhood where the residents were the "have nots" of the city. I was assigned to a route that was one of the worst sections of town, a street known as Ennis Alley. It was where the winos and prostitutes would hang out. The first day on that route, while walking through the valley, I became sick to the stomach. When I thought about how things were in D.C., I cried. Even at that low point, God let me meet people who would figure into what my ministry would eventually become.

One day I was on my route to deliver the mail when I came upon a tiny church where I encountered an elderly man sweeping the floor. I said, "You must be the pastor." He asked, "Why do you say that?" I replied, "Only the pastor would be doing this." We both laughed and he informed me that he was in fact the pastor, and that his name was Reverend A.D. Tucker. He invited me to his church, and when he found out my situation, he invited me to an association that would let you preach if you paid a dollar for dues. When it came my time to preach, I made the best of it. It was there I began to know pastors who had really small storefront churches. It didn't matter to me; I just wanted to belong.

It was on that same route I met a lady at a store on Northside Drive by the name of Lucille Parker. She became a part of God's plan for my ministry. My new pastor, Reverend M.L. Raglin, invited me to preach one Sunday morning, and the Holy Spirit was in the place. Mrs. Parker was a visitor to that church on that Sunday. She was so impressed that she told the deacons at her church that they needed to hear me preach, so they invited me to preach one Sunday morning. When I arrived at the church, it was love at first sight for me. It was a large church with many members, and a very spirit-filled church.

My first sermon at the Rising Star Baptist Church was entitled "Don't Tell Me – Show Me." The congregation loved it and kept inviting me back. I truly prayed for God to allow me to pastor that church, but I was to find out that even then, God was gently moving me toward the ministry He had already planned for my future. Even though the church liked me, politics entered the picture.

Daddy King, Martin Luther King, Jr.'s father, had been a friend with their now-deceased pastor. In those days, whatever Daddy King said in Atlanta was like the gospel.

He counseled them to not let the church leadership call such a young man, but told them that he had just the man for the church. He only allowed one name to be called—Pastor Charles Stokes—and in effect handed this man the church. I had never run up against anything like that, and I was brokenhearted. I was frozen out, not allowed by Daddy King to be considered. I felt the ultimate rejection and literally cried that night because it seemed so unfair.

During the time I was preaching in Atlanta, there was a singing group called the National Independent Quartet. One Sunday they were doing a concert and I asked who their musician was and if they needed one. I offered to play the guitar for them. They looked doubtful, but said, "Okay, let's try it." When I played, they were so impressed that they asked me to play for them when I was not preaching. That fit me fine because it was not like I had many preaching engagements. There was a member of the group whose name was Robert Owens, who would later become the first chairman of the board of a church that did not yet exist.

As in Washington, people just started following the group from place to place. It was Robert Owens that suggested to me to start a church, and because I had to leave the first church I pastored, the pain was still there. I did not particularly want to start another church. My desire was to have a church that was already organized.

When no offers to pastor came, I placed a fleece before the Lord and said, "If you want me to organize a church, let me see that their support is for real." I had paid my dollar to preach at the Southside Aid Association, and one Friday night it was my time to preach. I told them that if they were serious about starting a church, they would have to show up at the service. They showed up in good numbers.

I scheduled a night for organization at my apartment and asked Reverend A.D. Tucker to be our officiating pastor. I preached a sermon entitled "Consider Your Ways." I opened the doors of the church, and thirteen people joined. Our first offering was $15.00. Reverend Tucker then took over and his words were: "You now have a church that does not have a pastor. Who do you want for a pastor?" That night I was voted in.

When the news got out that I was organizing a church, the negative comments began to come in. One pastor sent me word that I was trying to start a church on singing. I went to my pastor and he advised me against it. We started out in a storefront. A deacon from the church once pastored by the late famed civil rights worker Reverend Dr. Ralph David Abernathy stopped by our storefront. He was a relative of one of my members, and he advised her that I didn't have good sense to try this.

One Sunday when I arrived at our little church, my members were upset, and I had enough spiritual strength to calm them down. I was teased at my place of employment daily and I was likened to the character "Rev. Leroy" in the comedy show of comedian Flip Wilson. Discouragement could not stop us; otherwise we might have given up after two months.

Mt. Ephraim Baptist Church Storefront at Haynes Street

When we were at the first storefront, I learned a lesson for life. That lesson was the fact that you may not have what you want, but you can at least be grateful for what you do have. The storefront had been rented to me by a minister who owned the building. One Sunday morning when I arrived at church, my few members were complaining about how they disliked the building, its location, and everything about it. Instead of me cautioning the members to be thankful for what we had, I joined in with them and I agreed that I would be so glad when we could leave that place. Sure enough, when I went to pay the rent, the owner told me we had to leave. Now we had nothing. Even though we were disappointed, the search for a new location began.

The only place we could find was another storefront building that was in a neighborhood which already had five well-established churches. This storefront was less than 500 yards from the Second Mt. Vernon Baptist church. I felt obligated to have a conversation with Pastor Baker explaining to him that it was the only place we could find, and we meant no harm. He was very warm and said, "If people want what you are doing, they will pass my church to get to your church."

Now as I reflect on this experience, another truth has become clear to me: as we trust God, we have an assurance that we will be successful. Within two years, our membership had grown from 13 members to 85. To me as the pastor, it was an endorsement from God that He had smiled on our congregation. As God has given us prominence in the religious life in Atlanta, it proves that God is still looking for people who are willing to step out on faith and begin to harvest souls. On the other hand, if God has not ordained the work, it will come to failure.

Before I was voted in as pastor, I had already prayed for a name for the church. I had opened the Bible and it fell on the word "Ephraim." I closed it again and opened it again and it fell on the word "Ephraim." So, I named the church Mt. Ephraim Baptist Church. The meaning of the word in the Hebrew means "double fruitful." We had no idea what God was doing. There was no one there but grassroots people who had no money, no great social standing, nor any great influence in the community. However, from that group came a church that would one day have a national television ministry, record many album projects that would go nationally, a ministry that feeds the homeless daily, a ministry in Ghana, and many other ministries, and a church that has grossed multi-million dollars per year. What a mighty God we serve.

The Theological Formation of R.L. White

One of my friends, the late Reverend Joe Hill, once asked me, "Where did you learn all the stuff you know?" We both had grown up in Macon, Georgia, but I went away to live in Washington, D.C. in 1963. I moved back to Atlanta in 1969, and it seemed to him that my knowledge had grown so much more than his. Although he had taken occasional trips, it became apparent to me that travel has much to do with the theology of a preacher (in other words, how God deals with His preacher).

You will remember that Peter, a faithful follower of Jesus Christ, was not able to look beyond his theology to include the Gentiles as a part of the religion of the Jews. To him, the Gentiles were barbarians because they did not follow the Jewish laws. Peter had a problem when it was suggested that the Gentiles would take on the Jewish religion. Peter was a Palestinian Jew who had never traveled outside of Palestine and he became the apostle to the Jews.

With the apostle Paul, it was different. Paul had traveled the world and had interacted with people who were from different cultures. He spoke several different languages and understood the many idiosyncrasies of different cultures. Therefore, he was more qualified to carry the gospel to the world, and he became the apostle to the Gentiles. What was the difference? He had been exposed to travel.

I attribute much of my personal theology to the many different travels that I have been blessed to undertake. Throughout my ministry, I have been blessed to travel often. Little did I know when I had my first real trip outside of Georgia that it would be the gateway to a ministry to literally millions of people.

As mentioned previously, I started a gospel group named the Mighty Wonders while living in D.C. We achieved a measure of success regionally, and we were able to travel to states like North Carolina, Maryland, New Jersey, Pennsylvania, New York, South Carolina, Virginia, and Georgia. Upon moving back to Georgia, when I joined the National Independent Quartet, that allowed me to go to more states where I hadn't yet been, such as Ohio.

When my ministry began to flourish, I had gained such a love for travel that I began taking our recording choir and interested members traveling to places they had never been. We were able to go to Los Angeles, California, as well as Indiana and D.C., just to name a few. One year, our church decided to send Lorraine and me on a cruise that took us to Saint Martin, 800 miles on the ocean. It is a quaint island that is half Dutch and half French. We also visited Bahamian Islands. While on this seven-day cruise, there was 30 minutes of inspiration that was facilitated by a Catholic priest. I told Lorraine I was insulted, and I said, "When we get back to Atlanta, I am going to book this ship and take a gospel cruise." That is just what I did. We sponsored a gospel cruise, and took with us the Pace Family, Albertina Walker, the Williams Brothers, and the Mount Ephraim recording choir.

It was an excellent cruise. When we stopped in Nassau, Bahamas, we cautioned everyone to be back on time because the ship would be leaving promptly. There were two ladies who were late, and we could not wait any longer. The ship began to disembark and when we saw them running toward the ship, the captain of the ship was asked to wait for them. The procedure for getting those that were late back on the ship was to hoist them up in some way. So they used something that looked like a huge tire innertube and pulled them up on the ship. It was so funny to me. To say the least, they were never late again. We rocked the boat.

My first real trip to Israel was theologically eye opening. Most of the preaching we do is based on the images we have formed in our minds from our experiences. When we landed, it was in Amman, Jordan. There were armed guards with guns on the plane. It was two weeks after Anwar Sadat was assassinated in Egypt, and Egypt was on our itinerary. We had to go through customs to get into Israel from Jordan, and because Egypt had a treaty with Israel, we had to fly over Israel to get back into the United

States. While on this trip, my whole theology was changed. For example:

1. I had thought the locusts and wild honey John the Baptist ate were grasshoppers, but I learned that there is a locust tree from which John the Baptist ate.

2. I had always thought that the stable in which Jesus was born was like a barn in the back of a house. In Israel it is a cave where you go underground and are protected from the weather.

3. I did not know that the Valley of the Shadow of Death referred to in Psalm 23 is an actual place. It is located on the edge of a mountain that made it very dangerous to walk on. One misstep could be one's death. Then I understood why David said, "Yea, though I walk through the valley of the shadow of death, I will fear no evil." It is truly a dangerous trek for one to take.

When we visited Egypt, we had to go across the Sinai Desert in a convoy because of the conflict between the nations that surround Israel. It is worthwhile to note that Israel is a little nation in the Middle East that only survives by its best friend, the United States. The USA needs Israel as a strategic country for refueling in war conflicts, as well as many other mutually advantageous benefits. The United States has armed Israel with very sophisticated weapons and has pledged to support Israel to the end. That is why you rarely find a politician speaking out against Israel. There is a strong Jewish presence and influence in this country, and our government is under close and constant scrutiny to make sure Israel is treated fairly in the conflict with Israel's enemies.

Our visit to the pyramids was also eye opening. We had requested a Nubian guide because she was black. She told us things you do not normally get to hear concerning the achievements of people of color. She took us to caves that showed how earliest man had a concept of God more than thousands of years before. We saw the Sphinx and also saw where its nose had been disfigured. We were told that it was an effort to destroy the fact that black people had created it. The pyramids were built by people of color who mathematically figured out how to build them to stand for hundreds of years without any glue or mortar. They are truly one of the wonders of this world. It is also interesting how Egypt is on the continent of Africa, but you don't get a sense of being in Africa. Egypt is bordered by the Mediterranean Sea, and because they intermarried with other races for so long, they now have lost most of their African features and do not seem to even want to be known as Africans.

One of the other sites we were shown was King Tut's grave. He was an Egyptian king who was not so prominent. He took the throne at age nine and died at age 19. When he died, they buried his gold with him. The gold was still there but Tut was gone. In other words, you can't take it with you. He also is thought to have been black. I have been to Egypt several times and it has been an educational and enlightening journey each time.

While I was in the seminary, at the Interdenominational Theological Center, being an older and well-known pastor, I was generally known as the pastor of the senior class and had a great relationship with members of the class. I would help them with the little things that came along with friendship. Two of the more enduring relationships were with Ben Colleton, now pastoring in Washington, D.C., and Ricky Holmes, who is now a Seventh Day Adventist pastor. Both became chaplains in the military and they extended invitations to me to minister in the Panama Canal Zone and in Mannheim, Germany, respectively. These were gratifying experiences. While in Germany, I had a chance to tour the place where Martin Luther nailed his 95 theses against the Catholic Church in 1517; this document began the Protestant Movement in Christianity.

Then there was my good friend, the late Chaplain Marshall, who was also military. He admired our ministry and started sharing tapes of my sermons with his Bible study group. This group became so impressed with my messages that they asked if I would come to Italy to share with them. I consented with one condition, which was that they would sponsor me a day in Rome, Italy. In my previous trips to the area, I had always wanted to go to Rome, but they could never get enough support to legitimatize a trip there, and each time they scheduled a trip to Rome it was cancelled.

The group desiring me to come scheduled a day in Rome for me and Lorraine. We were able to visit St. Peter's Basilica, which was so awe inspiring. While we did not see the Pope, the great buildings and the artistry of Michelangelo on the ceiling of the Basilica were breathtaking. We also toured

Valencia, where we saw the historic buildings, and for the first time we were able to witness streets that were made of water. We were given a tour of the military installation, where we were taken to a top-security room. There, we were shown how a military official could order an attack on a foreign country and they could watch the attack from that room. I was blessed by preaching in Italy.

Later I was invited to preach at NATO in Belgium, where we stayed in a chalet. On a Saturday morning, Lorraine awakened to what she said was noise. She threatened to call the front desk to complain. I looked out the window and said to her, "You may not want to do that." It was a musical group serenading the guests of the chalet.

We had a great time visiting foreign countries and getting a full knowledge of the different cultural traditions and religious practices in so many places. Our travels included different countries in Africa as well as Puerto Rico, Barbados, France, Dominican Republic, Mexico, and many other places. All these experiences have helped to impact my theological views. I can now say I have a more cosmological view of religion that helps me to respect other faiths and religions. I accept one's right to worship whomever one wishes to worship.

When I was younger, my theology only allowed me to accept the people who embraced Christianity, and I looked at others and felt sorry for them, as I said they were all going to hell. Now I am resigned to let God handle the judgment of where people will go in death. As for me, I hold to my Christian beliefs, and am committed to preach Jesus Christ, and Him crucified for the sins of the world.

He is my Savior, but I will not force my beliefs on others who choose to have other religions as their expressions of their faith. I hope this discussion on my personal theology affords one to see why my presentation of the gospel would be different than one who ministers never having left the state of Georgia.

CHAPTER FIVE

The Burden of Low Self-Esteem

The burden of being culturally deprived can be devastating to a child that has no idea of what is culturally missing until being exposed to other children. It was not until my father moved the family to Macon in 1955 that, for the first time, I was being exposed to children whose parents were able to buy them clothes that looked so good. When I was near them, I felt so unworthy. I never blamed my parents, because I knew they were doing their best. I just kept my feelings of being inferior to myself. It took courage for me to continue to perform in such an environment. All I could do was to daydream about how I would be on their level.

There were many things that reinforced my feelings of inferiority. When I began to notice girls, the ones I really liked showed little desire of having a relationship with me. I was small for my age, and my voice had not developed, I sounded like a girl on the phone. I had to convince them that I was a boy before they would believe me to talk with me. Things like going to the prom were out because no girl wanted to go with me. I remember getting a picture of a first cousin and telling people that she was my girlfriend.

When my aunt and her family would come from New Jersey, they would talk about how good life was for them, and I wished I could be like them. I never felt like I measured up. I always felt like the least of anyone wherever I would go. Life for me would never be better unless I began looking at myself as a worth-while person. There are so many things I wish I could have understood much earlier in my life. Things have never made more sense to me than now. Through this writing, I may be able to help somebody else who wants to see clearer how to make it through the pain.

I was one of five children in a family whose parents were struggling just to survive. They could not possibly have understood the emotional needs of their children, but it helped that they loved us and taught us many lessons as they understood life. These were valuable lessons that have stayed with me until today. They, however, could not understand why I had so much energy to get into so much mischief. Each day brought on new things to get into. You name it, I did it. I wanted to be good, but something seemed to drive me to think of things to get into. These things would bring me attention, though negative. I needed to help ease the emotional pain I was feeling but never understood as pain. Neither my mom or dad could understand me, nor did I understand myself.

My need for acceptance was so great that whatever it took to be accepted I excelled at it. Perhaps that was why I excelled at school. I was smart, and being smart brought me acceptance. There was not a boy or girl who could outperform me on anything. That's the reason why my elementary school teacher, Ms. Iris, caused me to skip a grade. My dad promised each of us a quarter if we would learn to recite the 66 books of the Bible. I learned them in record time. I am not sure my siblings ever learned them, but it brought me attention, and a quarter. While the quarter was a joy to me, the unseen need was attention and acceptance from my parents.

Now It All Makes Sense

My mother never knew the significance of what she was arming me with for a lifetime: the ability to sing. In our sibling group, the White Four, we achieved some notoriety in the circles where my family was known. This brought me feelings of acceptance. Even though my siblings liked singing, I was the one who excelled. At the age of six or seven, someone asked me to sing at a funeral and I sang "Jesus Keep Me Near the Cross." The undertaker, the late Hub Dudley, was so impressed that he gave me a quarter. To me, it was the greatest thing of my life. It was not the quarter so much as someone inspiring me to sing gospel songs. It was an important step that helped me to see as a child the need to view the gospel from a spiritual standpoint. God was the unseen hand guiding me to a destiny that He meant for me. I often realize everything I experienced in my early life was preparing me and putting me on track toward my ministry.

Predestination

Right here I think a discussion on predestination might prove helpful to the reader to understand my use of the word "destiny." The apostle Paul mentioned a biblical truth in Romans 8:29-30: "For whom he did foreknow, he also did predestinate to be conformed to the image of his Son, that he might be the firstborn among many brethren. Moreover whom he did predestinate, them he also called: and whom he called, them he also justified: and whom he justified, them he also glorified." This scripture is not true because Paul said it; Paul repeated a truth that already existed.

Another mention of predestination is found in Jeremiah 1:5, where the Lord says to the prophet Jeremiah, "Before I formed thee in the belly I knew thee; and before thou camest forth out of the womb I sanctified thee, and I ordained thee a prophet unto the nations." These two mentions in the Bible give evidence that there are those who are predestined for specific tasks by God. Jesus said in Matthew 22:14, "Many are called, but few are chosen." This statement is at the close of the parable of the wedding feast, when the king sends his servants out to invite people to come to a wedding feast but many of them were too busy to attend. Those who came were the chosen ones. In my humble exegesis of this parable, it is symbolic of those who accept the call of the Lord being the chosen ones who work toward the building of the kingdom of Jesus Christ.

Having related to these three Scriptures, it is my belief that there is a limited predestination that has a contingency based on what you do. Those who accept the Lord's call are the ones who are the called. My accepting God's call was known by God's omniscience and was preceded by God guiding my footsteps with different experiences that I would need in doing the work of the Master.

CHAPTER SIX

Ministerial Focus

I would suspect that most of the people in my craft, the preaching ministry, are the same way I was: concentrating on the art of preaching and not on what would eventually become the focus of my ministry. It took me a while to begin to understand the enormous importance of being personally aware of how precious the souls are that we are called to minister to and how, as pastor, my method of delivering God's Word makes a difference in the lives of those I am called to serve.

Different preachers have to decide on their style of preaching and their specialty. Just like medical doctors have their specialty, the preacher should recognize his/her strengths and weaknesses as well, in order to be effective as a servant of the Almighty God. I have also learned that it is necessary that preachers be willing to speak on any subject that helps the parishioners to grow in the Lord. I believe a pastor should not just preach something they heard somebody else preach about, but be deliberate and discriminating about what they feed the sheep.

If there is one thing that challenges every minister, it is to have a sense of what God expects of him/her as their assignment of presenting God's people back to Him in a more spiritually acceptable life. We live in a world that is essentially devoid of understanding about who God is and how children relate to their Creator. For me, one of the best things I could have done while my ministry was in its infancy was to begin to learn the problems faced most by the people God has assigned me to serve.

When Mt. Ephraim was less than four years old, I established pastor–member conferences. This has given me more insight as to how I should minister to our parishioners than any other thing that has affected my style of relating to God's people. These meetings were eye opening. People were dealing with issues like incest, domestic abuse, divorce, adultery, fornication, jail time, suicide, and murder. When these issues were brought to me, 1 quickly learned how much 1 didn't know about preaching deliverance to those who were captives of Satan's tricks.

One of the most import things in being a pastor is the ability to care about people you serve, those God has placed into your congregation. My late friend Reverend Moses Lee made an indelible impression in my ministry. I must have preached a total of 30 revivals for him. He had an unusual ministry. He pastored two churches, one in Vienna, Georgia, and the other at Springfield Baptist Church in Washington, Georgia. The problem was that these two churches were miles apart in distance and he lived in Atlanta. He would take Greyhound buses to the two cities on alternate weekends and come back late Sunday night.

When I would preach the revivals for him, we would stay at hotels in both towns where he pastored. Every day he would go to see every church member who was ill, shut in, or needed pastoral care. He would always leave a personal donation with each one. I saw how grateful his members were to see him. I would drive him to each home and I learned how important it is to let the members feel loved. Since Mount Ephraim is a megachurch, it would be impossible for me to take care of all the members and still be effective as pastor. Since we do a great deal of radio and television, our membership stretches across the whole metropolitan Atlanta area. It is difficult and almost impossible to do effective ministry without strategic planning. When I was not able to get to the homes of parishioners, I would sometimes hear the complaints about my not visiting the sick. The complaints bothered me.

I began to pray for an answer to this dilemma. When you are sincere in your prayers, God will give you an answer. Under the guidance of the Holy Spirit, I hired one of my associate ministers, Reverend Dr. Horace Andrews, to be our minister to the sick and to coordinate funerals. He served well until his health failed and he later died. Now Reverend Lee Franklin has become the minister to the sick and coordinator of the funerals.

The next thing I did was to begin to require our officers to visit the sick and infirm. We formed teams of officers that are on duty for a week at a time. We further organized the missionaries and the caring hands ministries to help in pastoral care. It has worked well. When life-threatening illnesses take place, then I personally make a visit.

With every meaningful experience God allows us to go through, it is another opportunity to become better pastors and Christian workers. I believe each significant experience with God helps to further my theology. So then, my working theology is that God gives a progressive ministry that helps us become more proficient in sharing our ministries to others, that we can be more successful in taking the gospel to a dying world.

CHAPTER SEVEN

Getting Over People Leaving the Church

One of the things a pastor must learn to do is to accept the fact that no matter how much you love your members, some of them will walk off and leave you. As a young pastor starting a church, with every new member that would join the church, I felt vindicated and that the Lord had spoken through me to the point I was grateful they chose to join Mount Ephraim. When somebody would leave, I took it personally, as if it were my fault.

There was a deacon of our church who joined as a deacon from another church. (I would honor that position if they came from another Baptist church.) Soon after he joined the church, he began to grumble and tried to undermine my authority as pastor. One Christmas season, he gave me a 100-dollar bill to help the less fortunate people to have gifts for the season, and he asked me not to tell anyone.

I did not have an easy feeling about the situation, and the next Sunday I told the church about it. His plan was to tell the congregation that he had given the $100.00 and that I didn't even announce it. When he made that declaration, everybody said, "Yes, he did." My suspicions had been correct.

I kept trying to work with him and he was just plain contrary. He decided to leave the church and I took it upon myself to talk him into coming back. I soon regretted that decision. He was a divisive person who kept stirring confusion all the time. Finally he left the church again. One thing 1 learned from this exchange was the fact that everybody in your life is not there for life. For some, when their season is over, you might as well let them go—as much as you may want things to work out, it will be in vain. When that season is over, regardless of how much you love them, they will leave.

People leaving the church was very painful until I began to question my own leadership. After a while, the Holy Spirit began to talk with me. He reasoned with me that if they left somebody else's church, it's likely that they would also leave mine. One of the things I believe is the fact that the majority of pastors/preachers are insecure because of the fear that they will be rejected. There is a tendency for pastors to watch the response to every sermon they preach. This is, as I see it, a dangerous practice, because there is temptation to cause the preacher to begin to tailor the sermon to the whims and desires of the members. Wanting to please people more than to please God is dangerous. This explains the insecurities we have; it is the fear of rejection.

Too often the pastors become people-pleasers rather than pleasers of God.

It is and has been my approach to being a pastor to allow God to give me messages that contain information, instruction, and inspiration. This is because the responsibility of the pastor is to be a source of Christian growth, which can only come through constant prayer to God to guide the message to the heart of the parishioners. This should be the aim of the sermon, instead of feeding the self-desire to please a listening audience.

I remember in 1978 when I went through a divorce while being the pastor of Mount Ephraim, as mentioned before. My greatest spiritual fear was members leaving the church because of my domestic failure. This situation was the source of my fears that people would reject my ministry. I found myself attempting to make sure I was pleasing the congregation with my preaching and pastoral care duties. I started trying to see who had significant influence with the members and believed that if I could keep them from leaving the church, the church would survive and my ministry would not be rejected.

The main person I fixed my attention on was the president of the Gospel Chorus. The Gospel Chorus was the largest auxiliary in the church and the president was a spiritual person and the members loved her. I believed if I just kept her, I would be fine. She had family in the church and was loved by the congregation. Unfortunately, this member came to me and said, "The Lord has shown me that I should move to another congregation." She gave me notice that the next Sunday would be her last Sunday. I was like

Job, saying to myself, "The thing I feared the most is come upon me." My fears became my self-fulfilled prophecy. I prayed to God to change her mind. On her last Sunday there, 12 people joined the church. I then realized the fact that regardless of who leaves you, if God is with you, your ministry is not dependent on keeping people in the church. Doing your best with integrity and love for God assures us that God will not leave us.

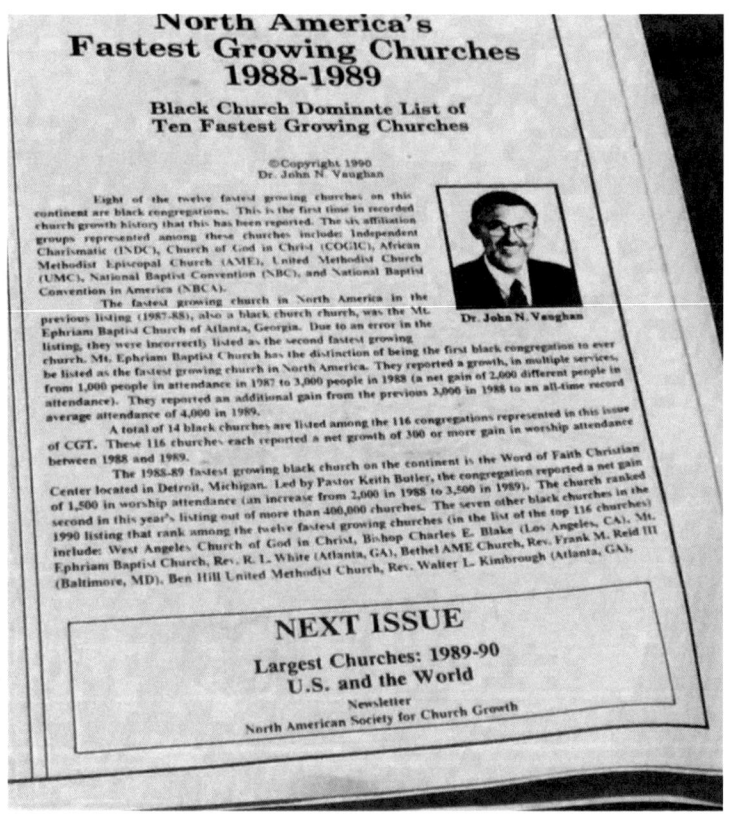

Fastest Growing Church in North America

From that time on, Mount Ephraim began an explosive growth period. By 1988 Church Growth America named Mount Ephraim the fastest growing church in the United States. We attracted more than 14,000 members. This year our church will celebrate our 50th year with a national streaming service, using all of the social media networks. A ministry in Ghana, West Africa, and many pastors who now have pastorates were birthed through our ministry. We have licensed, ordained, and mentored over 105 ministers of the gospel. I have endeavored, in writing this chapter, to show how the life of a pastor becomes a target of the devil himself. I am truly a witness to the fact that the pains of ministry can be challenging, but if one will hold to God's unchanging hands, God will have your back.

The whole issue of having people know about my domestic situation caused me much pain and my fears were many. I know now that God was molding and shaping me for a ministry that would be powerful in spite of my fears. Something pastors should watch is the trends of other ministries and the habits of the worshippers. One of the things one has to realize is that statistically speaking, seven out ten members that join a church will eventually leave it. These are facts that helped me in a class called Sociality of Religion at the Interdenominational Theological Center while I was working on my Master of Divinity Degree. Over the years, America has become more secularized and the movement has been away from the church. In Atlanta, 10:45 on Sunday morning was the church hour, and it seemed like everybody would be in church. As the years have progressed, and with the advent of religious cable television, the popularity of professional sports, shopping centers bustling with shoppers, and people viewing social media sites, the paradigm has shifted and the movement has changed; church attendance across the country has fallen to unparalleled lows.

Several in our city used to have 7:30 and 10:45 services, but now have combined services and are meeting at 9:00 a.m. I have mentioned these facts in order to help pastors and preachers understand that too many times, we blame ourselves for people leaving the church. That does not, however, relieve us from being the best we can be at winning souls for Jesus Christ. The preacher must make sure he/she has a relevant ministry and make use of the various social media sites that are available to us.

There was a time our church was on BET and the WORD Network that aired on national TV. It became so expensive (to the tune of almost $150,000 per year) that we had to come off the air. Recently I had been meditating on how we could begin a nationally aired telecast that has the possibility of reaching the whole world. Within a week after praying for this ability to reach millions of people, it was made known to me that Facebook was now facilitating church broadcasts. We have taken advantage of that media outlet and now we are everywhere.

Know Your Stuff

One of the things that has meant so much to my ministry is the statement "know your stuff." I have learned not to bring my own pains and hurt into a counseling session. One thing we should all do as pastors is to first recognize our own hurts. Sometimes our own emotional hurts run deep, and we can unintentionally bring our own pains to a situation that can cause it to be counter-productive. When that happens, you end up hurting more than helping.

When I say, "your stuff," I mean the painful things in your life that still hurt. When you are struggling with your own pains, there will be the temptation to give constructive advice, even when the thing you are advising someone on is the exact thing you are presently experiencing. Instead, your advice must be objective and not violate your own "stuff." There is danger in you becoming a part of the problem and losing your effectiveness.

I can now see how earlier in my ministry as a neophyte, I did not help situations when I attempted to, and I ended up being a part of the problem instead. For example, there have been some things I experienced in my domestic life that were very painful, and I was tempted to identify so closely with the person I was advising that I added my personal pain to theirs. We both were hurting at the same time and we became hurting partners as I lost objectivity.

Over the years, it has become clear to me that regardless of the situation, I must not tell a person, "Here is what I would do if I were you." If you tell someone to do something and it blows up in your face, then you expose yourself to the possibility of a lawsuit. Or even worse, your directions could cause more harm to a situation than good. Sometimes the situation you are asked to help with has already been spoken to through the Scriptures and you tell them to do according to the Bible. As a minister, we cannot demand our parishioners to do a certain thing, but must be careful to point out all possibilities of resolution to their problems because the consequences of their decisions must be left to them.

One of the first things they will ask is, "What shall I do?" You must emphatically state, "I can't tell you that," because they will need to be responsible for their own decisions. You cannot allow yourself to add "your stuff" to their problem. There are times when there is nothing you can do but to be present. I have learned that people do not always expect you to know everything, but just want to know that you are present, and that makes a difference.

On the other hand, there is what I call pastoral indifference, when families are going through grief and you fail to respond. One of the crucial times in the life of parishioners is when they are grieving. Whenever there is a loss or perceived loss, families go through grief—whether it is the loss of a close family member, a pet, a job, or a friend. There needs to be someone who can help them walk through their grief. They are not especially interested in hearing a sermon so much as they need the tender care of an understanding pastor.

I once was called to the home of one of my deacons, whose wife was in deep grief because her pet dog had died. Her grief was so profound, it was as if she had lost a human relative. For the first time, I became aware of the fact that people sometimes see a pet as a family member. Prior to that, to me a dog was not a human and no one would love a dog like they would love a human. I had to switch my thinking and counsel her as if her loss were a human. I don't know how successful I was, but not long afterward, she died. That gave me a new perspective on grief.

My experience in attending the seminary gave me new insights in pastoral care. As students, we were required to sign on as chaplain in a hospital or health institution. For me that was an insult after already pastoring for more than 30 years. We were required to have didactics, a requirement which was meant to give us more insight into our responses to patients. Our fellow students had to give their assessments as to why we responded to individual patients the way we did. We had to write verbatim the exchanges we had with selected patients. Our instructor gave us directions. I soon began to understand things about myself I never knew.

One of these eye-opening things about myself was pointed out to me by the instructor; it has had a major effect on the way I do ministry. She said only five words.: "I see you are manipulative." I was so puzzled about those words that I started assessing their truth in regard to how I behaved. Much of the way I had been doing ministry was to manipulate people into doing God's will by making them feel guilty.

I began to notice so many other ministries that are continually manipulative. When raising funds, they run a guilt trip on people who are not able or who don't really want to give to a particular cause. Many times these ministries reach their financial goals, but leave their parishioners in unsound financial situations because the people are guilted into giving funds they cannot afford to give. I had been guilty of this practice. I also had included some manipulative statements in my messages that were designed to inflict guilt on those who were listening to my sermons. I had tried to manipulate patients in the hospital setting into becoming closer to God. In reality, God does not need us to run guilt trips on people to make them do His will.

I have learned the fact that if you preach the gospel without using "your stuff," God will do the convicting, if the gospel is preached according to His will. In my counseling, I became acutely aware that I should never tell people exactly what to do, but to make sure the counseled person knows what the will of God says and help them to see the ramifications of their choice. I must be deliberate in making sure they understand the decisions are theirs and not mine. There is another reason as well: if you advise someone to do a certain thing in their personal situation and the advice turns out to cause someone to be tragically killed, maimed, or otherwise harmed, you can be sued for malpractice.

Some states now require a counseling pastor to comply with the laws of the state before claiming to be a counselor. God forbid that one should be arrested or be sued while earnestly trying to do the will of God out of ignorance. There are so many ministers and lay people who have good intentions. Some decide they want to go into hospitals and randomly go into rooms and preach their brand of religion. In my own experience, one of my spiritual sons had no training in how to pray a "hospital prayer," so he prayed as if he were in his whooping Sunday morning message. Hospital staff and security came running, and other visitors were curious. When they wanted to know what was wrong, the reply was, "He is just praying." No wonder some hospitals have stopped people from visiting without express requests from patients. I hope this discussion on knowing your stuff causes the reader to seriously take a look at how they do ministry.

CHAPTER EIGHT

Women in Ministry

If a pastor is not truly in touch with self, that pastor can stumble into some things without intending to be there and it can be very dangerous. At the top of the list is the subject of women. If a pastor is emotionally insecure, he can be a prime target for "women trouble." As a young minister/ pastor, I stumbled into some situations I never wanted to be in and now as I look back, I can say, "I can't believe I did that." A great deal of young preachers who start preaching think that all they need to do is to be able to put a good sermon together, and if he does it consistently he may get a church. But I have found out that pastoring requires a minister who is in touch with himself; if he isn't, he may end up reacting to things in a confusing way.

Anyone who thinks they cannot be tempted is setting himself up for a supreme temptation by the enemy. Satan never gives up on causing trouble for the pastor. One thing the pastor has to look out for is women who are drawn to power and when what they see in the pastor is what they wish they could see in their mate, they will sometimes transfer their affection to the pastor. There are others who are just lonely, and they will idealize the pastor and make a play for him. At other times, if the pastor himself is emotionally starved for affection, he can make the sad mistake of believing in his own irresistibility. The attention he is receiving is the result of women seeking to be tied to someone they consider to be the kind of man they want. This type of woman will sometimes try to entrap him and have him for herself, even if he has a wife.

One of the phenomena of African American churches is the fact that women are the overwhelming majority of parishioners and can be counted on to help advance the work of the ministry in which they serve. Often the women are young. Women are generally attracted to power and they see power in the pastor. Many do not have that positive power in their husbands or mates. When the pastor is also good looking, even though he is married, women in the ministry will admire him and many times they will allow themselves to idealize him, and in some occasions, they will transfer their affections to him without realizing it. The problem is, sometimes when they are in their home environment, they will talk about him in glowing terms. If their mates are insecure, they may begin to envy the pastor and will sometimes put him under close scrutiny.

The pastor's wife seems to have a built-in radar and can sense it when a certain woman seems to be getting too available and flirtatious with the pastor. The pastor sometimes like the attention, and many times becomes uncomfortable when he has to interact with her. His wife then becomes uncomfortable when he has to interact with her, becoming increasingly irritated with her also for being attractive as she is seemingly being seductive.

Sometimes the wife will begin to resent the lady and when it is time for the pastor to be approached by the wife, because he knows the wife is watching, he tries as fast as he can to get away from her. I have had many experiences when the women are too friendly and many times I have prayed when certain women approached me, especially when I have stood to shake everybody's hand. I have been so uncomfortable in such situations when having to interact with eligible females. I have sought to minimize the anxiety by helping my wife see that while in the congregation, I am operating in a different role as pastor, trying not to be short and trying not to alienate the young attractive woman who has many family members in the church.

Many times, the issue of women in church can be volatile if the pastor is being victimized by women being "catty." They are often aware if his spouse has a problem of being jealous, and many times they will do things they know will upset her just to get on her nerves. Sometimes they will make a pass at the minister just to cause friction in his family relationship.

Many times the pastor can bring peace to the marriage by spending more time with his family, constantly showing his love and attention toward the family. It can make a positive difference. Many times, however, if he secretly enjoys the attention he is getting from other women in the church, it is a sign that he may be in danger of an ego that convinces him that he is a powerful man when so many times the women are more attracted to his power than his appearance. I know so many preachers who get caught up with their self-image; they are unwise as they unwittingly allow themselves to get caught up in multiple relationships. Many times these pastors are hurting within, and they get some satisfaction from the attention from the opposite sex.

After being in ministry for 51 years, I have had just about every type of experience with females that one can have and many of them have caused personal pain, some have caused problems, some have become friendships, and some have become a personal test of my willingness to stay grounded in the ministry. When there are serious issues at home, it can cause serious issues in the ministry. I found that out the hard way.

There was a time when my marriage was seriously in question and it was a painful situation for me because I felt like I was being mistreated. It is easy to be tempted when you feel like there is no peace at home. It seems like someone else can be so understanding. An affair brought much peace to me, to the point that I felt like giving up on my marriage. My wife was also considering a divorce. My love for the church and, most of all, for God Himself caused me to beg God for mercy because I knew I had a marriage that seemed on the rocks and another person who was ready to commit to me. Somehow the new person decided that if I were not going to leave home, we were through. She in fact spoke the words that broke it off. The pain of having two relationships both on the rocks was a position I had seen and advised others how to handle.

Whenever you get to the point that you are broken, this is the time when the Bible gives the best advice.

Suddenly Proverbs 3:5-6 took on a new meaning for me. "Trust in the Lord with all thine heart and lean not to thine own understanding. In all they ways acknowledge him and he shall direct thy paths." I am a witness that there are times you can put your personal pain even before God Himself without knowing what you are doing. I began to call on the Lord to bring me some peace. God heard my prayer and began to take charge of my life as He had done before. I was a broken man. God began to show me that He was able to heal the pain, and He began to do so. Thanks be to God, He began to open my eyes to what was happening in terms of being wrong on my part.

The hurt between my wife and me was very painful, but the Holy Spirit began to show me how to turn back to my wife even though she had not changed her position. My prayer changed and I began to get the Lord to help me turn back to my home. Slowly he allowed my mind to turn back to my home. The Lord showed me that my calling meant more than a personal peace that I thought I needed. Today, even though there has not been a great change on her part, God has brought us closer than we ever have been.

I have made myself transparent because I know from experience how the devil can make right seem wrong and wrong seem right. I know many pastors who have been (and some still are) where I have been. I am a witness that we can all be led astray by the pains we feel as pastors. I would think seriously before making a decision to either leave home or promote a new relationship. As the late blues star Johnny Taylor would say (tongue in cheek), "It's cheaper to keep her." Never give up your prayer life. Today I thank God because He held me steadfast and wouldn't let me go.

Why I Have Always Supported Women in Ministry

In almost every book I have written, I have always included a chapter concerning women in ministry. This book will not be an exception. I was reared in a culture that has traditionally not believed in women in ministry. My mother was a strong supporter of my father's ministry. She became so close to the Word until she felt the call to preach the gospel. Because my father had been taught all his life that God does not call women to preach, he rejected her call and because she wanted to keep the family together, she never publicly announced her call to ministry.

The call was so heavy on her life, she would have all our playmates come and sit on the front porch while she would teach biblical lessons. It got to the point she would teach them twice a week, and she did not have to make them come. I have even met successful ministers who have given testimonies that she taught them Bible while they were young. She would teach Sunday school in almost every church my father pastored. She died believing that she had let God down because she never publicly announced her call to preach the gospel. I do thank God that she made a difference in so many lives while she "preached" in the name of teaching. I can still remember some of the things she would teach us as little children, things that I still cherish today.

Even as a child, I thought it was so unfair to keep these women from exercising the gift that God had called them to do. When I entered the Washington Baptist Seminary in Washington, D.C. in 1968, there was a woman minister in my class named Violet Ankrum, who had a keen sense of missions. I admired the way she was not intimidated by the males in the class who rejected her ministry.

The seed that was already planted by my mother began to grow in me, and I began to search for the theological reasons that men would be so vocal in their condemnation of women in ministry. Most of the time the men would quote the Scripture where the apostle Paul said that a woman should not speak in the church, nor to usurp authority from a man (1 Timothy 2:12). As my exegetical skills began to evolve, the way I interpreted those Scriptures was in a different light. I began to contextualize the Scriptures and I began to understand that the apostle Paul was addressing discipline in a church that had been victimized by women who were causing havoc in the church. His directive to the women was to be quiet in the church.

I further found that the term "usurp authority" meant that the women should not take over by force in the church. Then I reasoned that if a man gave the authority to a woman, then it was not a case of usurping. To usurp authority has the connotation of seizing authority by force. People who usually quote Paul's directives to women in the church to not speak often seem not to deal with the fact that Paul's directives to women were only temporary, but his permanent view on women was the fact that he said: "There is neither Jew nor Greek, there is neither bond nor free, there is neither male nor female: for ye are all one in Christ Jesus" (Galatians 3:28). A clear exegesis of this Scripture suggests to us that God is not a respecter of persons. In other words, God calls who He wants and when He wants.

Women Can Be a Blessing to Ministry

Just like women can be a hindrance to a marriage, they can be a blessing to a marriage. God still has some women who are spiritually strong enough to have a platonic relationship with a minister, women who can be a friend without bringing a sexual meaning to a relationship. Many ministers lose their ministries because of women who mean them no good. What we as ministers must begin to understand is the fact that we are in spiritual warfare and the enemy, Satan himself, wants to cause trouble in the spiritual life of the preacher. Believe it or not, there are women who have the desire to bring down any preacher they can.

One thing the preacher too often does is fail to recognize the fact that women talk to each other and sometimes will play games. However, there are some women who are a blessing to a ministry. Some are unattractive, and some are beautiful. They love the Lord and they serve as platonic friends whose fervent desire is to get close to God. They will befriend the preacher and warn him of such plots that could become a detriment for a wonderful ministry. I have known such friends in my ministry and they are still friends today. They are godly enough to be true friends who can understand spiritual warfare and remain strong enough to help a troubled preacher. I am fortunate to have some in my ministry who were not interested in a sexual relationship, but used their God-given gifts to be witnesses for the Lord.

Some theologians theorize that Priscilla, who belonged to Aquilla, was attractive and Paul had an attraction for Priscilla. Whether true or not, she was by all estimation an asset to Paul's ministry, who was an excellent witness for the Lord. The perennial weakness of the male ego is to sexualize a relationship, but thanks be to God, the Holy Spirit will guide a preacher through the trap set by the devil.

I have known some women who genuinely wanted to be a friend to a pastor's wife, but the wife is so insecure that she questions the woman's motives. A few women have warned me about tricks formed by the enemy, Satan, whose desire was to bring the ministry down, but they have been used by God to be an asset to ministry, not with fanfare but because they loved the Lord. These serve as guiding angels to the growth of the pastor and God has allowed them to be a blessing to the ministry.

I think it would be a good thing to note that some ministers unfortunately do not understand the fact that the emotional baggage they bring to a relationship may predispose them to become traps to their own ministry. If, for example, a man's emotional past has been one wherein relationships with women have been disappointments and he has tried to compensate by having multiple relationships within or outside the congregation, he may be unconsciously trying to satisfy his own failings. He may be constantly getting into multiple relationships to attempt to satisfy a damaged ego that cannot be satisfied. He may still be searching for the perfect person to bring him satisfaction for his damaged ego and may cause heartaches to many women, especially his wife. Too many times the preacher is spiritually misguided by the enemy himself, whose desire is to destroy a ministry. I counsel many preachers and try to help them become strong enough to know their own weaknesses and not become a detriment to their calling.

In the last days, God will pour out His Spirit upon all flesh, and our sons and daughters shall prophesy. When you look at the etymological meaning of the word "prophesy," it means to tell forth, or preach. There are other instances in the Bible that present a good defense for women in ministry. One is when Jesus met the Samaritan woman at the well. We are all familiar with that encounter. When the encounter was over, she ran and told the men to "come see a man who told me all things that I ever did" (John 4:9). The Bible testifies to the fact that the men believed her, and many will be in heaven because they believed on Him. Suppose the men had rejected her message; they would not have been saved. I believe that one of the reasons there are controversial issues in the church is the fact that some Scriptures have been taken out of context.

It is ironic that before my father died, God called my sister to preach, and because she knew Dad's stance on women preachers, she was afraid to tell him. When she told me that she was afraid to tell Dad, I asked her, "Was it God that called you, or man?" When she finally told Dad, he said that God had already shown him that. I noticed that he was softening up when my wife, Lorraine, answered her call to ministry, and she was invited to preach at his church for Women's Day. The Holy Spirit moved so powerfully, he said, "I am beginning to reconsider my stand on women preaching." It was so fitting that my sister would have to assist him in the pulpit before he died. He also lived to see my sister Ethel organize the Move Mountain Ministry, which is thriving; my wife, Lorraine, who is a powerful preacher in her own right; and my daughter Patrina, who has been led into a prison ministry for the past 25 years. She also has a ministry for associate preachers throughout Atlanta.

I do have to confess that when I moved back to Atlanta in 1969, the sentiment against women preachers was so strong, I wanted so much to be accepted, that I adopted the same stance on women in ministry as others. Whenever a woman would tell me she was called to preach, I would channel her to the missionary unit. There was a woman who wanted to answer her call, and I attempted to send her to the missionary unit; however, she would not allow me to skirt the issue. She made me face it. At a board meeting, I made the announcement that "our first female minister would be preaching her initial sermon and those of us who don't believe in women in ministry, stay home." That was 30 years ago and now it is no longer an issue at Mount Ephraim.

To me, the whole issue of the role of women in church needs to be reexamined. While I did not start out to be a spokesperson for women in the life of the church, I have continually defended my stand on women in all phases of the worship experience. Almost half of the 55 officers on the official board at our church are female. For the first time, we have a woman who is the Chair of the Official Board. Many churches have a deaconess board and the requirement to be a part of that board is she has to be married to a deacon on the deacon board. Yet I refer to Phoebe, the deaconess mentioned in the Bible. She was not a deaconess because her husband was a deacon, but she had the same authority as her male counterparts.

There are certain churches within our denomination that have viewed my stance on women in ministry with skepticism, some chauvinists who refuse to worship at Mount Ephraim, some who refuse to sit on the pulpit with women in ministry even though our ministry is one of the largest ministries in Atlanta. I thank God for allowing me to deal with the whole role of women in ministry in a positive way, and many ministers have sought my advice on how to allow females to have a place in the ministry of Jesus Christ. I do not question other churches and their policies and neither do I refuse to worship with them. I just tell our female ministers not to go against the rule of certain churches. If the pastor does not allow women in their ministry, I do not challenge him; I ask our female ministers to remain in the audience when we visit their churches.

I am aware that it is hard to convince people who have believed a particular thing all their lives to embrace a different way of viewing a situation within their belief system. I believe that many things in the faith statements of different denominations are inaccurate, but because of pride, there is a reluctance to challenge some if these inaccuracies in favor of not upsetting those whose friendships they cherish over intellectual and spiritual honesty. I believe they do their own followers theological damage that hinders spiritual growth of those who trust their leadership.

When my wife Lorraine and I were engaged with a religious leader in this discussion while we were entertaining a group from England, the discussion ended up in our being invited to England. This discussion involved the issue of doctrinal beliefs of their faith, such as the exclusion of women in ministry and other things that we saw as wrong to teach. Before the end of the conversation she acknowledged the fact that many of the doctrinal beliefs that undergirded her denomination were wrong, but to admit so many years of wrong, and changing afterwards, would be a personal crisis if people would lose the respect they had for her. She would rather keep teaching these things than admit how long she had taught the wrong thing. I have often wondered how many people who are in spiritual leadership have continued teaching things they knew to be inaccurate for personal reasons.

Whatever someone believes should be the result of spiritual growth and intellectual honesty; however, I have settled with this conclusion: a person should be able to theologically explain why they approach ministry in a certain way. After 51 years in ministry, my approach is to constantly reevaluate the things I have taught as truth, and whenever a new truth is revealed by the Holy Spirit, then that truth should be embraced. I earnestly hope those who will read this book will be helped by this discussion.

Dr. R. L. White, Jr. and Evangelist Lorraine Jacques White

Growing Older in Ministry

There is an inevitable change that every pastor and every layperson will have to face: growing older gracefully. I believe a pastor has to know when God is saying it is time to move on. In some denominations, the pastor has a mandatory age for retirement. Other pastors lead congregations that have not been progressive in their thinking to plan for his future. When the pastor needs to retire but does not have the finances to live at the same level he/she currently lives at, these pastors find themselves trying to continue pastoring when their effectiveness has diminished. I have known pastors who have had the tragedy of a sickness that forces the end of a great ministry. I have seen churches force a pastor out, and they are forced to leave with a broken heart.

Make no mistake, this question has forced itself into my mind as the years have kept adding up. The one thing I have learned is the fact that the pastor must be able to hear what God is saying in the midst of what everybody else is saying. I believe it is a tragic mistake for the pastor to listen to someone other than God. I don't believe God has a mandatory retirement plan. I further believe God will speak to each of His servants individually, just like God calls us individually. There is a tendency to judge ministry by the world's standards and look at age without hearing what God is saying. I truly recognize that ministry is looking toward younger people partially because of the way our culture handles its aging population.

In other cultures, when a person reaches the degree of being considered advanced to the norm, they are honored and placed in a position of prestige and can live out their lives with a position of honor. Too often I have seen ministers die with broken hearts because of the insensitivity of the people they have served with honor for years. For me, it becomes a dilemma when younger ministers try to position themselves to take over the minute a pastor shows signs of aging. For years now, I have had preachers try to get on my good side in hopes that I will recommend them to take over when my pastoring days are over. It happens so often that I struggle when preachers become so friendly and act like they genuinely respect what I have been in their lives. Others have been bold enough to ask me to be sure to place them in position to take over when my pastoring days are over. I have struggled now for years to hear what God is saying over the noise and clamor of people who have no clear understanding of how God still speaks to His servants.

Recently I have celebrated 75 years of age and 51 years of preaching. I constantly watch for the signs of my ministry weakening to the point that I do not want to become a hindrance to the growth of the church. So, recently I thought I would respond to the unanswered questions in everyone's mind, "When is he going to retire?" I decided to put minds at ease and during my birthday celebration I was going to say: "I am asking God for five more years of pastoring," but before I could even make that announcement, the Holy Spirit spoke to me in an unmistakable voice that said, "The God that was wise enough to call you is wise enough to tell you when to stop." I have found peace in those words because I love the Lord now even more than I did when I received His call. I firmly believe God will help me to know when I have reached my day of retirement from the pastorate, but I know I will never retire from preaching. The reason I have undertaken this subject is the fact that so many of my friend pastors struggle with the same decisions.

When I look to the Scriptures, I notice how God spoke to Moses to turn the mantle over to Joshua, Elijah to Elisha, and David to Solomon. There was not a record of Solomon having a clear word from God as to who should succeed him. I believe Solomon had fallen in such disfavor with God because he allowed all his wives and concubines to bring their little idol gods with them when they became his wives. The fact displeased God to the point that it affected Israel in a profoundly negative way. Maybe Solomon forgot the way that he had made an agreement with God for wisdom to lead God's people. There is no profound word in his writings as to how God wanted him to the pass down his leadership after his demise. This fact is borne out by the way his sons fought over the question of who would lead Israel after Solomon. History shows that this question was answered in the fact that Israel was plunged into a civil war that resulted in Israel being divided into two kingdoms, the northern kingdom and the southern kingdom.

I happen to believe that God, who never changes, still speaks to His servants when they keep in fellowship with Him. I have placed my future in the hands of Him who called me. In the first place, my prayer is that I will be able to discern His voice as I did when He calls me.

I thoroughly believe that the older a preacher or pastor gets, if one allows God to talk with him as he did when he leaned on God earlier in life, God never withdraws from any of us who cherish our relationship with Him. The problem is when the pastor has fought so many battles that he gets tired. When the pastor loses that enthusiasm he once had, his mind tends to start looking for the members to allow their desire to have someone younger. He begins to monitor all their comments and their way of relating to him as a sign of how they are turning against him.

I had a friend who was an excellent pastor; his congregation loved him. I preached many revivals for him. We had grown up together. He sang with a gospel group as well. His group was the Spirit of Harmony. His name was Reverend Joe Hill. He had an infectious personality that made people love him. His decline started when his domestic relationship with his wife began to decline. He overheard his wife talking with another man in what amounted to phone sex. It was common knowledge that everyone believed his wife was not good for him. They separated and eventually she divorced him. At that time he came to me for advice. He was concerned that his church would reject his ministry.

His congregation loved him enough to keep him. In the meantime, his wife changed her mind and wanted to get back together. Again he asked my advice. My advice to him was, "If what caused you to break up still exists, it would do no good to go back." He made up with her and they got back together. Sadly things had not changed and he was in the same place. The judge talked to him in a very harsh way and he felt helpless to help himself. He was not able to overcome the hurt and anger he felt, and it started working on his mind to the point that he began to feel like people were turning against him.

During the last revival I preached for him, his sons in ministry knew how close we were and asked if I would meet with them to help convince him that nobody was against him. We agreed to meet after church on a Tuesday night. I followed through with his spiritual sons and when I made my presentation along with them, he responded, "You all are against me too." He said to me, "If you are not against me, let me come do a revival at your church." I told him that I would allow him to preach on a Sunday morning. His response was "I want to preach a revival." When I left town, a group of his other friends took up an offering and brought him to Atlanta to a psychiatric clinic, but in two or three days he was back in Macon. He had signed himself out.

Sadly enough, within a year he died. I was preaching revival in Shreveport, Louisiana, but left early to attend his funeral. This whole episode showed me that the pastor will be attacked by Satan himself and unless he practices the same things he has been taught for years, Satan gets the victory. From time to time I think of him and this tragedy and consider the negatives that have plagued me in life. They make me more determined than ever to hold to God's unchanging hand. I am determined to let nothing separate me from the love of God. Many are the afflictions of the righteous, but I am convinced that in everything God is with me. My advice to pastors who are under attack by the enemy is to be strong in the Lord.

In 51 years of ministry, I have seen so many pastors go through agonizing situations, and those who prevailed have been rewarded with long ministries and the glory of God has been on their side.

I have preached all over the USA, in Germany, at the Panama Canal, in South America, Africa, Italy, England, and Israel. I have baptized three times in the River Jordan, where Jesus was baptized. I have preached in Belgium, visited France, and attended conferences in Bermuda, the Dominican Republic, and Puerto Rico. I have counseled people of color in third-world countries and perhaps places I cannot remember during the 51 years God has allowed me to preach the gospel of Jesus Christ. The point to this revelation the Holy Spirit has just given me is the fact that sometimes God has already given us more than we dreamed of, and because we are going so hard in another direction, we don't even recognize the fact that we should be praising God for making our dreams come true. It is for this reason I profusely apologize to God for my inability to recognize how precious His blessings have been to me. Today, I have found more reasons to praise God, not boastfully, but humbly, for all His benefits to me. Thank God for opening my eyes. At a time when most pastors my age are retired or thinking about retiring, I am excited about the next ministerial blessing God has in store for me. All praises to the glory and honor of the Almighty God.

CHAPTER TEN

Caught in the Middle

Many times young ministers make serious mistakes while meaning to do well. Such mistakes can be costly; however, once they are made, the lessons are lifetime messages. After about four years as pastor of Mt. Ephraim, there was a murder in our church family. It was a husband/wife situation. I had never dealt with the legal aspects of ministry, and the police came to take a statement from me. I thought being cooperative was the best thing to do. I shared all I knew about the situation, especially since I had been counseling them, only to find out the prosecutor planned to use my testimony to convict the husband for the crime.

I was distraught because his side of the family said if I were called to testify it would further incriminate him, and they wanted it to seem like it was the wife's fault or they were going to leave the church. God knew my love for both of them because of my closeness with the family. It was a time of agony for me. I cried many nights over the situation. When I received orders to appear as a witness for the prosecution and I knew they planned to use my testimony to convict him of murder, it was an especially emotional time for me because the victim was my best friend. She was wealthy and owned a store. She credited me with leading her to Christ and she would often say, "When I die, I am going to leave money for the church, and as long as you are there, the money will be there, but if you ever leave the church the money goes with you." She was the one who helped finance my first album sermon project entitled "Now Run and Tell That." She was a real friend. The one thing I had not understood is the fact that God would never have left me alone.

On the day of court, I purposely arrived late and sat in the back of the courtroom. When they called my name, I slowly went to the witness stand and with the first question, God brought something back to my memory and that was the fact that anything parishioners tell you in confidence, you as pastor cannot be forced to tell in court. With the first question, my deliverance came when the attorney asked me, "Have you ever counseled the accused or the victim?" I quickly said, "Yes." The attorney asked that my testifying be invalidated, and the judge agreed. God had answered my prayers and I quickly left. I have learned that if you believe in what you preach and trust in the God who called you, God will never let you down.

Poisonous Things to the Ministry

If there is one thing I have noticed since I have been in ministry, it is the fact that a preacher can do enormous harm to his own ministry. One's actions as a preacher can be the main reason his ministry is dead. I thank God for the fact that my father was never caught up in a scandal before he died. All of us preachers have done something that is worthy of bad publicity if we were exposed even in the smallest way. As I see it, we can kill our own ministry in three ways: 1) failure to study, 2) if we allow pride to take over, and 3) if we allow rotten eggs to rot in our lives.

Not all preachers have been fortunate to have gone to a seminary or academy. I have noticed the fact that young preachers are hungry for knowledge. God has allowed me to go to many states and even to foreign countries, but many preachers have not had the advantage of having the funds for school. Perhaps there is no school of religion nearby, and there are no good role models for them to follow. There is a tendency for preachers to listen to other preachers and copy their styles and methods.

Every preacher who wants to be successful in ministry must have a good source of information that is a reliable fountain of truths according to the proper exegesis of Scripture. Since the advent of social media, some preachers watch TV evangelists without discrimination concerning the truthfulness of gospel presentations and end up spreading alien doctrine. Others have not become well versed enough to use the internet to attend a religious school online. Going to school on the internet can be a valuable tool for preaches who live in remote areas. If a preacher leans to his own understanding without having gone to a school of higher learning, it will hamper his ministry. If he relies on the same messages too long, people will begin to reject his ministry because of stale sermons. Having to deal with the same body of literature (nothing new has been written in the Bible in over 2,000 years), the preacher must lean on the Holy Spirit to keep his/her preaching fresh. The reason we call the Bible a living document is because each time you read a certain Scripture, you should have a different message derived from the current doctrine taught by your own denomination. This fact can help the preacher spot inconsistencies in certain ministers he admires, and this can be a form of study. But finding a creditable organization of study can have an amazing effect on your ministry. Failing to seek new ways of presenting the gospel message can be deadly to a ministry.

Allowing a rotten egg to kill a ministry has to do with an experience I had at our church. A mysterious foul smell started to stink up my study. In spite of looking all through the trash, and in the dining area, we couldn't find it until our attention was drawn to several cartons of eggs that had been placed in my office for safekeeping to be used in our homeless ministry. We began to examine each carton of eggs and at the bottom of all those eggs there was one egg that had been broken, which had started to rot. That one little egg was the culprit of stinking up my entire study and the relaxation area in the church. That was a lesson for me. We may sometimes become proud of the fact that as ministers, we live lives that we think are unspotted by sin.

It doesn't have to be something big to destroy your ministry. Sometimes it's a little thing: not calling someone who is ill, little habits that people don't know about, a look of pride because of the ministry God has given us, looking over people, mistreating one's family, secret relationships nobody seems to know about. Sometimes it is just something as small as a rotten egg, but the wrong attitude about the "little things" we do can ruin a thriving ministry.

In my moments of contemplation, I can never get too comfortable with the little rotten eggs in my life. I am convinced that one's attitude has a great deal to do with how you feel about the little rotten eggs in your ministry. You can never get to the point that you try to give people the impression you are so holy they think you are almost perfect. I recognize the fact that the ministry God gave me doesn't thrive just because of me. I am grateful to God because He looked beyond my faults and saw what I can become. God's grace and mercy have kept me these many years—not because of my righteousness, but by His grace.

As I am happy that my father never fell victim to a scandal, I am also grateful that God has kept me within the bounds of His grace.

CHAPTER TWELVE

The Relationship Between Senior Pastor and Associate Minister

Since I come from a family of preachers, naturally the issue of other preachers in the same ministry has come up often. I have to admit that I was somewhat skeptical of the relationship with my associates, particularly because I have witnessed a pastor who entrusted his congregation into the hands of an associate when the pastor got in legal trouble and was sentenced to a little more than a year in jail. The trusted associate split the church and started his own church right across the street from the home church, taking as many members with him as he could.

Regarding my associates, I wasn't always as secure as I should have been; I became suspect of other preachers that could really preach. I was always wondering if these preachers had an agenda. Did they want to take my church? I had an elderly minister friend, the late Reverend A. Tucker, who helped me immeasurably when he told me, "If the people love and want you, somebody can come by and preach the bricks out of the walls, but when they get through, your church still wants you." I never told him but he really helped me for the rest of my ministry, even though I did envy the gifts of some preachers who came through. This issue has come up many times in my ministry, and I had to first deal with who I am as a pastor.

I had to understand the fact that God gives us all our special spiritual gifts for kingdom building. This kind of insecurity taught me how people who are insecure in their relationships feel when they feel threatened. It is a fear that one is not able to measure up to others and is inadequate when it comes to being compared to someone else.

One of the problems I see in our Missionary Baptist churches is the fact that as respected preachers, pastors, and administrators, we do not train our associate ministers that there are many other ministry duties that are important. The local associate minister should be aware of the fact that he doesn't have to be a pastor for his role to be appreciated just as much as the pastor's role.

In our denomination, we believe in the call to preach by God Himself and when one acknowledges the call, his first responsibility is to have a full conversation with the pastor. At that time, the pastor should have in place some procedures to help make sure the call is real. We should have some requirements in place that an aspiring preacher will have to follow other than just hearing someone say that "the Lord has called me to preach."

There should be established procedures that one should have to go through before being admitted as a minister of the gospel. Right now the pastor grants the aspiring preacher an initial, or trial, sermon. After the initial sermon, the newly called preacher should be fully taught the doctrine of the church and what role the newly called preacher plays in the ministry of the church. My procedure is when one says to me "I have been called to preach," I will not at that time schedule a sermon. I ask for an explanation of why that person believes the call has been made by God. I then make the person aware that for six months, I will not even mention the subject again.

Six months later, it is that person's duty to reaffirm the call and I do not schedule an initial sermon for up to another six months. This means that my procedure takes up to a year. One would be surprised as to how many who have announced the call come to the conclusion that it was more of a desire rather than a call by God, and they abandon the claim to have been called by God to preach the gospel.

Too many preachers are in a hurry to get ordained without a full knowledge of what being ordained really means. Some think they should be ordained within a certain period of time, as they believe that they are not advancing in their ministry as they should be. Too many preachers become so insistent on being ordained that if the pastor doesn't schedule an ordaining ceremony, they feel that their ministry is being held up and will go seeking for a pastor who will fast-track their being ordained. However, this does not mean that they are now a successful preacher.

One of my suggestions is that Baptist churches and pastors should develop a process that all pastors should consider. What happens now is each pastor haphazardly leans to his own understanding. Many times I am ashamed to admit that we have allowed some people to enter ministry whose actions prove that God had nothing to do with their calling. We soon witness that their attempts are met with utter disaster. Over the last 40 years, I have regretted helping some enter ministry who should never have been called. The problem is, it is difficult for us to tell people that God did or did not call them to preach. We need to build some criteria to help us have a better sense of accomplishment when someone enters ministry. Too often we have allowed people to enter ministry out of our pity for them, even when we know they are not there yet.

The results of our not being more deliberate in demanding more from those entering ministry is the fact that the Baptist Doctrine has been diluted and there are preachers being called as pastors who have no idea of what we believe as Baptists. I suggest that the following criteria should be required before one enters ministry:

1. Be familiar with the Articles of Faith in the Baptist church.

2. Be able to discuss the Baptist Covenant.

3. Be able to intelligently discuss their own conversion experience.

4. Be able to discuss incidents surrounding their divine call to preach.

5. Be knowledgeable of Scriptures.

6. Know the difference between the Old and New Testament.

7. Know what a licensed preacher can or cannot do.

8. Know what an associate minister should or should not do.

9. Yield to the leadership of the pastor.

10. Never engage in the negativity of members in the church concerning the pastor. While there may be some rejection on the part of some pastors, it could help shore up some of the peace in the local church.

CHAPTER THIRTEEN

Ministry as President of the NAACP

One of the last things I expected was to be president of the NAACP. My whole life was impacted by my knowledge of this great group that was born at a time when this country was getting ripe for the great civil rights movement. I was living in Macon, Georgia, while segregation was in full practice. I experienced having to go to the back doors of restaurants in order to be served because we could not eat in the same room with white people. At that time, there were many restrictions on what we could do. We could not live in the same neighborhood with white people. The dividing line for colored people was the railroad tracks. It was where the pavement ended and the dirt roads were prevalent. They presented many problems in our neighborhoods. I remember many times when it rained how our cars would slide into the ditch and people would have chains in their cars so they could pull people out of the ditch when the rains would come.

My life was punctuated by having been limited by the prevailing racial injustices and it was a silent dream that one day 1 would be able to do what white people could do. It was then 1 heard about the NAACP and Dr. Martin Luther King, Jr., who was spearheading the civil rights movement that was beginning to bloom. Ms. Rosa Parks refused to move when she was ordered to give up her seat on a bus in Montgomery, Alabama, and was subsequently arrested. Dr. King was pastoring in Montgomery and was reluctantly convinced to lead a movement to protest the segregation practices in Montgomery. It was there that boycotts began to take place, spreading all over the South.

The black people in Macon caught on with the spirit of opportunities that were only available to white people. The public transportation was provided by the Bibb Transit Company. The majority of the riders were black, but there were no black bus drivers, nor were there black managers that were a part of the transportation industry. The demands were made: removing signs that indicated colored people must seat from the rear and whites seat from the front, black drivers to be hired, and promotion of blacks to positions in management.

There was opposition to these demands, so we boycotted the transit system. 1 would get up early in the morning to take my mother to work. In just a few days, we brought the whole system down and our demands were met. We would have mass meetings in the churches for an assault on segregation wherever discrimination was practiced.

Opposition to black schools being given inferior educational material was the order of the day. The white people were fighting us at every front, as if we wanted so hard to have integration just to live with them. The point was made that we were not so in love with living with white people, but we had a right to if we wanted to. I was deeply impressed with the NAACP and became a part of this group in 1963. That same year, l moved my family to Washington, D.C. and the issues l had been a part of were not the same, so the seeds of liberation for my people went dormant.

In 1969 when my job transferred me back to Atlanta, those issues were the same as when I had left the deep South, and I again became involved, but more as a financial supporter. Each year I would make sure the church would support the cause by giving $1,000.00. l will never forget one evening in 1998. I was in Columbia, South Carolina, preaching revival, when a call came in for me. It was the legendary Executive Director of the Atlanta NAACP, Jondelle Johnson. She was well known in civil rights circles in this country. I thought she would ask for some financial support, which l was prepared to give. However, that was not what she wanted. She said that she had called to ask me to run for president of the Atlanta branch of the NAACP. I immediately started to tell her about my very busy schedule. Her reply was, "l will do the majority of the work. I just need somebody with a good reputation to lead our branch." l responded that I would think about it.

When l had not called back in two weeks, she called me again and pleaded with me, and l finally said yes. I told my father I was running, and he never said a word. Deep within I knew he didn't want me to run because of his painful past dealing with racial discrimination and having heard how civil rights leaders were harmed. But by then 1 was committed to run.

I prayed to God that if 1 were to run, 1 would win, but if not, it was fine with me. I told the church I was running and for the most part, the church support was positive. On election day, I won with 74% of the vote. To be honest, 1 was a bit overwhelmed to be elected as president of the branch where the late Julian Bond, President of the National Board of the Directors, the famed Andy Young, national figure and former mayor, as well as former mayor Maynard Jackson, Hank Aaron, and many well-known figures were under my leadership.

While it was a prestigious position, it was also very challenging with many problems and little money. There were many times when moments of accomplishment gave us joy, but many times our efforts were rendered vain as we were not able to successfully make a lasting change in the fight for justice for people of color. Once 1 became president of the branch, it became clear that there was a disconnect between the goals of the NAACP and the perception of the larger part of our race, which is that the NAACP is no longer relevant in today's time.

It was my belief, and still is, that racial discrimination is alive and well, and to try to disparage rather than become allies with any group that has the common goal of fighting racial discrimination is a sad mistake. One of the tactics of those who disagree is seen in communists, which is to "divide and conquer."

CHAPTER FOURTEEN

The Issue of Pastoral Care

One of the most effective ways of making sure people will be endeared to one's ministry is to be deeply concerned about the people one is called on to serve. Too often younger ministers graduate from the seminary, or just have a talented way of presenting the gospel, to the point that people will herald their educational achievements or their ability to "pull it." However, there are those who tend to rely on these wonderful gifts given by God to automatically assure themselves of success. I even know of preachers who spend their time working on the most poetic way to say things in order to get the response from those who listen to rise to explosive proportions. Then there are others who spend much of their time working on their whoops. To be sure, it is admirable to be able to excel in these areas, but there will be a tendency to forget one of the most dangerous things a pastor can do, and that is to neglect pastoral care.

One would have to know that after 51 years of preaching, and meeting preachers of every calling, I have learned much about successful pastors. Some of the most successful pastors I have known have not been the greatest-known preachers, but they have been some of the most serious pastors. They have been intentional about preaching messages that nurture the growth and maturity of parishioners. When the members are constantly fed with growth-oriented messages, one can begin to see the spiritual growth of the congregation, which is one barometer to monitor. A second barometer is to be concerned about the story of each parishioner. Each member you meet has a story and if they are willing to share their storms and pain to the pastor, he shows he cares by remembering their pains. His care becomes evident when inquiring about their well-being. So many times people need to feel significant; when the pastor shows concern, it communicates care. An even more telling sign of pastoral care is being present and available when there is sickness or death in the families of his members.

Having preached revivals throughout this country, one of the most painful stories I have heard has been about pastors who show little care about those whom they serve. There is much truth to the traditional saying that until a new pastor has shown real pastoral care, he is considered an outsider. People are perceptive and they can tell when your care is genuine. When the pastor has passed the care test, he becomes the pastor in their hearts.

In my own ministry, I have never been known as a great preacher because I have never majored in the art of preaching. There are preachers who major in the art. People come from near and far to hear them. Other preachers major in their ability to mesmerize the listener with the use of words, often speaking over the heads of the people.

For me, my emphasis has been a ministry of healing and reconciliation aimed at the spiritual and emotional healing of the parishioners. I thank God for this because the meteoric growth of Mount Ephraim has been due to the caring ministry. One of my spiritual sons, Reverend Willie Coombs, was invited to preach at a church in Savannah, Georgia. Ministers were in the study talking about great preachers. The pastor, not knowing that Reverend Coombs was one of my spiritual sons, made this comment, "R. L. White ain't a helluva preacher." Coombs was insulted and asked him, "Have you ever been to the 8:00 a.m. service at Mount Ephraim? He has a full house twice a day and they are not coming to hear the choir sing." The pastor was noticeably quiet. I have come to the conclusion that if a preacher allows the Lord to use him/her, then God will guide the emphasis and content of their message.

If a pastor has been in the ministry for any period of time, there are some things that can ruin or destroy his/her ministry. After being in ministry over 51 years, I can truly say that if a preacher can finish his/her ministry without being affected by a scandal, it is a blessing from God. If you are being effective in ministry, as effective as you are, the amount of temptation is equally as treacherous as success is. Tests by the enemy himself will never stop coming. When you think you are not as vulnerable to temptation as you used to be, that is when you are a prime target for the enemy Satan.

As you get older, the temptation changes and you have to be careful not to think of yourself as being invincible. There are some things that can destroy your effectiveness as a pastor. I have witnessed many pastors make some disastrous mistakes and it is by the grace of God that to date I am still standing, not because I deserve to be, but God has kept me when I didn't deserve to be kept.

A Call Within a Call

One of the things I have learned about the call to ministry is the fact that each preacher must find out his/her specialty within the call. I have been around preachers all my life and I have come to appreciate the different styles and unique ways that each preacher approaches ministry. Some preachers are especially gifted with the ability to mesmerize their audience with their poetic style, and some are gifted in a way that will constantly amaze the audience with their presentation of the gospel. Some are great lecturers, teachers, and use the style of staying with the text. Some have a unique way of whooping and emotionally lifting people into the presence of God with joy. I encourage preachers to find out what their gift is, and excel with humility.

How does a minister recognize his/her specialty as a preacher called by God Himself? I believe that God orchestrates different experiences uniquely in preparation for effectiveness of ministry. It has been said that locked away in your memories is every experience that you have ever had. These different experiences shape the way a preacher goes about doing ministry in the area of expertise used to carry the gospel. In my own ministry I have been able to recognize the many gifts that the Holy Spirit has given me to be effective as a pastor.

Past Experiences Are Preparation

When I look back over my life, I can see that my experiences are part of what I have become as a minister to God's children. I am now convinced of the fact that at each and every experience in my life, God was preparing me to be a more effective servant that would bring more children of God into the kingdom of Jesus Christ.

The home and circumstances into which I was born were substandard. The chance for a Negro child to rise above these conditions were almost nonexistent. My earliest memory of life was at the age of six years old, when I experienced a disappointment that would prepare me to deal with future disappointments in life. By the age of 12, I would sell newspapers that nobody was interested in. It was the *Pittsburgh Courier*. Along with that I would sell Blair Products, which included deodorant and facial cosmetics. I am now convinced that the people who purchased these articles from me only did so to encourage me in trying to help myself. This in fact was training experience in how to be a seller, which would many years later result in selling Jesus Christ to a dying world.

At the age of 14, I started shining shoes at the Moon Barber Shop in Macon. If I did a good job, the shoeshine would be 15 cents and if I did a really good job, I would get a dime tip. In those days, there was someone called the Chattanooga Shoe Shine Boy, who could make the shoe shine rag sound like a train. I learned how to do that and it brought me even more tips. When I was a student in school, I was often teased about my clothes. This too was painful, but God taught me how to excel in knowledge above the other children and that resulted in my skipping a grade in school.

There is a term that sociologist call "compensatory." Since I was small for my age and without knowing it, I used that to cause me to learn how to sing better than the other children. I was not known for my sports ability. I often made public recognition for my singing. This was a training for me to one day teach people the fact that you may not have the ability others have, but God can bless you in spite of what others think. As I seek to think about the names of those who rejected me in my childhood, most of them never rose above their circumstances, yet God still has kept blessing my role in life. The lesson in this is "use the hand you are dealt, and you can excel."

My life became a love for gospel singing that pushed me to start a teenage gospel group with my sister and teenagers in the community. This group, called the Angels of Heaven, became well known. Because our musician often wouldn't show up, I bought an old guitar for four dollars and all day, every day, I practiced until I began to play fairly well. I eventually became the musician for the group. This element of being determined in our mission was preparing me to teach others that there is always a way, even when Satan would try to discourage us.

Regardless of what group I was in, I was always the manager. Being the manager required me to handle the bookings and secure a way to get to the programs. Whatever came up, it was my job to work it out, even though most of the time I was the youngest one in the group. I had no idea what God was doing. Now I know that I was being called by God to become a gospel preacher who had already been trained in the minutest ways to become an effective minister of the gospel. I would be called not only to spread the gospel through the state of Georgia, but through the United States and throughout many countries internationally.

At one point, for years I was on the BET Network, well known throughout the world. I later appeared on the WORD Network, which aired in 105 countries. Before that there was a radio station in Nashville, Tennessee, that we could be heard on in 38 states. It was, for many of us, the only station where we could ever hear gospel singing late at night. I can remember when WLAC would fade out on the air waves, then bring it back up. I considered it a great thing to hear myself broadcasting on this great station and becoming friends with the great Hossman. It was also a thrill for me when I went to Bermuda to watch my broadcast in that great area. Today at our church, we live stream and use Facebook Live on Sundays, and wherever there is a satellite, our church can be seen and heard all over the whole world. Thanks be to God.

I believe the more radical one's faith in God, the more one can accomplish in the kingdom of God. Average faith produces average results. Above-average faith brings about above-average results. But radical faith brings about extraordinary results. In order for the amazing results that have come through our ministry, it has taken radical faith.

From the time I was five or six years old, my mother taught me to sing. She never knew she was providing the inspiration in this little boy who was destined to become a prominent voice in the world of the gospel of Jesus Christ. I praise God for my mother, who now rests in the arms of God. My dream has always been to travel everywhere talking about the Lord in song. My dream was nurtured by my love for gospel singing, and when I would watch the famous recording groups come to my hometown to sing, I thought there was no calling any higher than being able to travel with a gospel quartet.

It has taken years for me to recognize the fact that God had a higher calling that would exceed that. In the ministry God has given me, I have been able to organize two churches. The Mt. Siloam Baptist Church of Washington, D.C. that eventually failed when I moved back to Georgia. The minister I left in charge lacked the effort it took to keep it going because it was more than he wanted to do. In Atlanta, the Mount Ephraim Baptist Church has been the fastest growing church in the United States. When asked the question if I believe in predestination, I have a limited view, and that if one elects to do the will of God without reservation, it can be traced back to every significant experience in one's life. That's why I named this chapter, "A Call Within a Call." To God be the glory.

Endorsements

Out of Nothing is a compelling, authentic, historic, and inspiring account of an exceptional man's extraordinary walk with God. The life story of Dr. R. L. White, Jr. should, and I believe one day will, be read as sacred literature. Like David, he is generously honest about his humanity. Like Abraham, he is consistently bold with his faith. Like Joseph, he is genuinely humble with his dignity. Like Samuel, he is gracefully insightful with his spirituality. And yes, like Jesus, he has a deep, abiding interest in the holistic welfare of people.

On the surface it reads like a tale of a spiritual superhero; an almost mythological modern spiritual leader whose professional singing talent, prolific gospel album recordings, undeniable charisma, preaching experience, academic achievements, pastoral success, social justice advocacy, global television ministry, and kingdom celebrity status would keep him on the short list of America's most elite pastors. Yet, somehow, Dr. R. L. White, Jr. comes across as a national treasure hidden in plain sight by his own humility and simplicity, two of the rarest character traits among men of his stature.

This autobiography goes far beyond the surface of his giftedness and accomplishments to provide a behind-the-scenes look at a once broken man who totally trusted God to make something of his life, even "out of nothing." From the nothing of poverty, racism, low self-esteem, professional rejection, and personal failures, God took a "snotty-nosed boy from the rural back roads of Georgia" and raised him to a level of success and prominence that could only be explained by great faith and Divine Providence. From 13 people, $15, apartment living room, storefront buildings, to a multi-building campus erected within a seven-year span worth a combined eight million dollars. From a man denied a pastoral opportunity by one of the fathers of Atlanta's civil rights movement to becoming the longest-serving president of the Atlanta NAACP. God made him more than just something. God made him someone special to me and tens of thousands of others who are blessed to call and know him as Pastor.

Therefore, I highly recommend this book to believers and nonbelievers alike; rich and poor people alike; preachers and lay people alike; and to anyone who seeks to experience in our own lives and ministries God's power to make something "out of nothing."

Reverend Renard D. Allen

Pastor, St. Luke Missionary Baptist Church

Dayton, Ohio

Dr. White's reflection and testimony is a message that is original and inspiring to the soul's spirit. It reminds us that with God all things are possible. "Little becomes much when God is in it." To God be the glory for the man and the message.

Reverend Dr. Douglas E. Stowers

Pastor, Mt. Calvary Baptist Church

Atlanta, Georgia

Out of Nothing by the Rev. Dr. R. L. White, Jr. scales significantly towards a new plateau in recognizing and understanding the pendulum of Divine Providence in our lives, through the lens of his humble beginnings in segregated Macon, Georgia, to become founder and esteemed pastor of one of the first megachurches in Atlanta. A foremost authoritative theologian and illuminating civic and civil rights leader for over 50 years, Dr. White eloquently brings home the message of what Jesus assured the Apostle Thomas, "I am the Truth and the Way." The book succeeds magnificently at showing us how the confluence of love, wisdom, temperance, and endurance allows us to live brilliantly as children of God. You will cheer for saints and sinners alike who come away assured there are blessings to be had when they are able to Let Go and Let God. You won't have to read far to have the confidence of the fearless eagle flying in a storm. With powerful wings, the eagle flies towards the storm, taking advantage of the very storm that lesser birds fear and take cover from. Dr. White shows us that we too can have powerful wings like the fearless eagle—Faith and Hope—if we only believe.

Rev. Edward R. Davis, Jr.